Foreign   JUN 13

HARRAP'S

Bulgarian phrasebook

Mira Kovatcheva
Christine Milner

Mc
Graw
Hill

New York Chicago San Francisco Lisbon London Madrid Mexico City
Milan New Delhi San Juan Seoul Singapore Sydney Toronto

ISBN-10: 0-07-148627-5
ISBN-13: 978-0-07-148627-9

McGraw-Hill books are available at special quantity discounts to use as
premiums and sales promotions, or for use in corporate training programs.
For more information, please write to the Director of Special Sales,
Professional Publishing, McGraw-Hill, Two Penn Plaza, New York, NY
10121-2298. Or contact your local bookstore.

Editor & Project Manager
Anna Stevenson

Prepress
Heather Macpherson

CONTENTS

INTRODUCTION

This brand new English-Bulgarian phrasebook from Harrap is ideal for anyone wishing to try out their foreign language skills while travelling abroad. The information is practical and clearly presented, helping you to overcome the language barrier and mix with the locals.

Each section features a list of useful words and a selection of common phrases: some of these you will read or hear, while others will help you to express yourself. The simple phonetic transcription system, specifically designed for English speakers, ensures that you will always make yourself understood.

The book also includes a mini bilingual dictionary of around 4000 words, so that more adventurous users can build on the basic structures and engage in more complex conversations.

Concise information on local culture and customs is provided, along with practical tips to save you time. After all, you're on holiday – time to relax and enjoy yourself! There is also a food and drink glossary to help you make sense of menus, and ensure that you don't miss out on any of the national or regional specialities.

Remember that any effort you make will be appreciated. So don't be shy – have a go!

ABBREVIATIONS USED IN THIS BOOK

adj	adjective	*n*	neuter
adv	adverb	*pl*	plural
f	feminine	*sing*	singular
m	masculine	*v*	verb

PRONUNCIATION

PRONUNCIATION AND INTONATION

After every phrase given in Bulgarian in this book, you will find the pronunciation given in italics. If you follow these phonetic transcriptions, which have been specially designed for English speakers, you will be able to make yourself understood in Bulgaria.

Be sure to put the stress on the syllable where the vowel appears in **bold** type. Getting the intonation right is crucial, as giving prominence to a different syllable can change the meaning of the word: for example, *govori* means "he/she is speaking" but *govori* means "speak!" – a different function altogether. Most compound words have two stressed syllables, for example *fotoaparat* (camera).

ALPHABET

Bulgarian uses the Cyrillic alphabet. A recently introduced official system for rendering Cyrillic characters in the Roman alphabet defines how names and place names are to be transliterated. This table shows the letters of the Cyrillic alphabet (upper and lower case), their equivalent in the Roman alphabet and their pronunciation. The final column shows the transcription used in this book. As some Bulgarian sounds do not exist in English, we have used codes to transcribe them.

Cyrillic	Official Norm	Name	Pronunciation	Transcription
А а	a	*a*	*a* as in *far* but shorter	*a*
Б б	b	*buh*	*b* as in *bar*	*b*
В в	v	*vuh*	*v* as in *very*	*v*
Г г	g	*guh*	*g* as in *go*	*g*
Д д	d	*duh*	*d* as in *do*	*d*
Е е	e	*e*	*e* as in *pet*	*e/eh* (in final position)

Ж ж	zh	zhuh	s as in mea*s*ure	zh
З з	z	zuh	z as in *z*ebra	z
И и	i	ee	*i* as in *fi*t; when stressed *ea/ee* as in *ea*sy/ch*ee*se	i/ee (stressed)
Й й	y	ee kratko	y as in Ma*y*[1] or *y*es	y
К к	k	kuh	k as in *k*ing	k
Л л	l	luh	l as in *l*ion	l
М м	m	muh	m as in *m*eet	m
Н н	n	nuh	n as in *n*et	n
О о	o	o	o as in *o*ff[2]	o/oh
П п	p	puh	p as in *p*op	p
Р р	r	ruh	r as in *r*ed (the r should be rolled)	r
С с	s	suh	s as in *s*even[3]	s
Т т	t	tuh	t as in *t*ip	t
У у	u	oo	oo as in p*oo*l	oo[4]
Ф ф	f	fuh	f as in *f*ire	f
Х х	h	Huh	ch as in the Scottish lo*ch*	H[5]
Ц ц	ts	tsuh	ts as in si*ts*	ts
Ч ч	ch	chuh	ch as in *ch*eese	ch
Ш ш	sh	shuh	sh as in *sh*ow	sh
Щ щ	sht	shtuh	sht as in ma*shed*	sht
Ъ ъ	a	er golyam	u[6] as in p*u*rr	u/uh
ь[7]	y	er maluk		y
Ю ю	yu	yoo	u as in *u*tility	yoo
Я я	ya	ya	ya as in *ya*hoo	ya

1 The "i kratko" is not a stand-alone letter. When it comes after *a*, *e*, *o* or *oo* it changes their sound to *ay*, *ey*, *oy*, *ooy*, or it comes before *e* and *o* to give *yo*, *ye*.

2 When *o* is stressed the lips are more rounded than in English. When *o* is not stressed it is rounded even more and approximates the sound *oo*, eg the word for milk, **мляко**, is heard as *mlyakoo*. This peculiarity is very important for hearing but is not reflected in our transcription.

3 The Bulgarian *s* is always pronounced as *ss*, not as *z*.

4 We have used the transcription *oo* to distinguish the sound from *u* which is reserved for "er golyam" (ie as in *pool* versus *purr*).

5 We have identified *h* in the text with the symbol *H* to avoid any temptation to pronounce it like an English *h*. It is a hard sound unknown in English but approximate to a Scottish or German *ch*.

6 A widely used vowel, frequently seen transliterated as *a* but the sound is not so open. In final position when stressed it is conventionally written as *a* but the pronunciation is preserved and we still transcribe it as *uh*: **в града** *v graduh* "in the city".

7 This letter doesn't stand alone; it is used in combination with *o* after a consonant to produce the same sound as *yo*, eg **шофьор** *shofyor* driver.

Vowels

When *e* comes at the end of a word it is never pronounced *ei* as in English *café*. To remind you of that we transcribe *e* at the end of a word as *eh*, eg *leteeshteh* airport.

In words like **наем** (rent) or **трамваи** (trams) two vowels follow one another but are never read as one sound. To remind you to pronounce such vowel sequences as two syllables and to distinguish between a fused and a non-fused sound (*moozey* museum but *mooze-i*, plural), we have inserted a hyphen between the two vowels: *na-em* and *tramva-i*.

Consonants

Six consonants change their sound when they come at the end of a word and within the word when they come before the other consonants *k*, *p*, *ch*

and s, t, f, ts, ch and sht. It is a hardening of the sound, which means that:

b becomes p: хляб hlyap; общо opshto
v becomes f: лев lef; евтино eftino
g becomes k: бряг bryak; рогче rokcheh
d becomes t: град grat; сладко slatko
zh becomes sh: гараж garash; ножче noshcheh
z becomes s: ориз orees; разписание raspisani-eh

There are two short words written with just one letter: в v in and с s with.
We have attached them to the following word in the transcription since
this is the way they are pronounced. As described above, в changes its
pronunciation from v to f when it comes before voiceless consonants:

в гаража vgarazha in the garage   в колата fkolata in the car
с тебе stebeh with you   в София fsofiya in Sofia

When these prepositions come before a word that begins with a similar
sound they double up so that в becomes във and с becomes със:

във Франция vuf frantsiya in France
със сестра ми sus sestra mee with my sister

Double consonants
It is important to note that when two identical consonants follow one
another within a word, usually -ии- or -тт-, that both consonants are to be
pronounced as separate sounds and not to drop one as we would in English.

Simplification
In some cases where there are several consonants in a row that would
confuse the English reader we have simplified the pronunciation as
Bulgarians themselves do: чувствам се choostvam se (rather than
choofstvam se).

EVERYDAY CONVERSATION

Watch out for "yes" (**да** *da*) and "no" (**не** *neh*): confusingly for pretty much everyone else in the world, Bulgarians shake their heads for yes, and nod for no! So if you are speaking to someone and see them shaking their head, it probably means they agree with you... However, some people may try to do the opposite when they realize you are a foreigner. If you get confused, ask your question again and add **да или не?** *da ilee neh?* (yes or no?).

Bulgarians are very tactile – they shake hands not only when meeting someone for the first time but every time they see them. With closer friends the handshake will probably be replaced by a kiss on each cheek or a hug for men. It is not uncommon to see girls or women walking down the street arm in arm or holding hands. If you're unsure which greeting is appropriate it is probably best to take your lead from your host.

People you meet for the first time should be addressed using the polite form until they start to talk to you using the informal **ти** *tee*. Having said that, many young people now address virtually everyone in this way, and if this happens there's no reason to keep up the polite form. Generally speaking, Bulgarians don't expect foreigners to know their language and are delighted at any attempts to speak it. Any mistakes will be forgiven, even calling someone **ти** *tee* when you should be calling them **вие** *vee-eh*.

As in English, to be polite you should always remember to say thank you (you can get away with the French word *mersee* as it is a lot easier to pronounce than **благодаря** *blagodaryuh*). There are also various expressions of courtesy: one you will hear a lot is **заповядайте** *zapovyadayteh* (polite/plural form) or **заповядай** *zapovyaday* (informal singular form). This is used when giving someone something and can be translated as "here you are" but can also mean "you're welcome", "take a seat", etc. Expressions of good wishes are also commonly used, for example: **всичко хубаво** *vseechko Hoobavo*, which could be translated as "all the best".

да си жив и здрав/да сте живи и здрави *da see zheef ee zdraf* (masculine informal/formal), **да си/сте жива и здрава** *da see zheeva ee zdrava* (feminine informal/formal), **да сте живи и здрави** *da steh zheevi ee zdravi* (plural), which literally means "be alive and healthy" and is another way to wish people well – for example on a name day or birthday.

честит *chesteet* (masculine), **честита** *chesteeta* (feminine) or **честито** *chesteeto* (neuter), meaning "congratulations" or "happy", as in Happy Birthday **честит рожден ден** *chesteet rozhden den*, Happy New Year **честита Нова Година** *chesteeta nova godeena*, Happy Name Day **честит имен ден** *chesteet eemen den*. You can also say it to someone who has bought, for example, a new suit, car or piece of jewellery: the word changes according to the gender of the item ("suit" is masculine, "car" is feminine, "piece of jewellery" is neuter). It is followed by the phrase **със здраве да го носиш/носите** *suz zdraveh da go nosish/nositeh* ("may it bring you good health").

The polite form of asking for something: I would like **бих искал/бих искала** is less frequent than the straightforward I want **искам** and for this reason this format has been used in the phrasebook.

The basics

bye чао *cha-o*
excuse me извинете *izvineteh*
good afternoon добър ден *dobur den*
goodbye довиждане *doveezhdaneh*
good evening добър вечер *dobur vecher*
good morning добро утро *dobro ootro*
goodnight лека нощ *leka nosht*
hello здравей *(sg)*/здравейте *(pl) zdravey/zdraveyteh*
hi здрасти *zdrasti*
no не *neh*
OK окей *okey*, добре *dobreh*
please моля *molya*, ако обичате *ako obeechateh*
sorry! прощавайте! *proshtavayteh!*, извинявайте! *izvinyavayteh!*
thanks, thank you благодаря *blagodaryuh*, мерси *mersee*
yes да *da*

Expressing yourself

I'd like ...
искам да ...
*ee*skam da ...

we'd like ...
искаме да ...
*ee*skameh da ...

do you want ...?
искате ли да ...?
*ee*skateh lee da ...?

do you have ...?
имате ли ...?
*ee*mateh lee ...?

is there a ...?
има ли ...?
*ee*ma lee ...?

are there any ...?
има ли ...?
*ee*ma lee ...?

how?
как?
kak?

why?
защо?
zashto?

when?
кога?
koga?

what?
какво?
kakvo?

where is ...?
къде е ...?
kudeh eh ...?

where are ...?
къде са ...?
kudeh sa ...?

how much is it?
колко струва?
kolko stroova?

what is it?
какво е това?
kakvo eh tova?

do you speak English?
говорите ли английски?
govoriteh lee angleeyski?

where are the toilets, please?
къде е тоалетната, моля?
kudeh eh to-aletnata, molya?

how are you?
как си *(sg)*/как сте *(pl)*?
kak see/kak steh?

fine, thanks
добре, благодаря
dobreh, blagodaryuh

thanks very much
много благодаря
mnogo blagodaryuh

no, thanks
не, благодаря
neh, blagodaryuh

yes, please
да, моля
da, molya

you're welcome
няма защо
nyama zashto

EVERYDAY
CONVERSATION

11

see you later	**I'm sorry**
до скоро	съжалявам
do skoro	*suzhalyavam*

Understanding

внимание	attention
вход	entrance
запазено	reserved
изход	exit
не работи	out of order
не... /недейте да ...	do not ...
отворено	open
паркирането забранено	no parking
пушенето забранено	no smoking
свободен	free
тоалетни	toilets

добре дошъл *(m)*/**добре дошла** *(f)*/**добре дошли** *(pl)*
dobreh doshul/dobreh doshla/dobreh doshlee
welcome

един момент, моля	**заповядайте, седнете**
edeen moment, molya	*zapovyadayteh, sedneteh*
one moment, please	please take a seat
има	**имате ли нещо против да ...?**
eema	*eemateh lee neshto proteef da ...?*
there's/there are	do you mind if ...?

как си *(sg)*/**сте** *(pl)*?
kak see/steh?
how are you?

какво правиш *(sg)*?/**какво правите** *(pl)*?
kakvo pravish?/kakvo praviteh?
what are you up to?

лек ден
lek den
have a nice day

PROBLEMS UNDERSTANDING BULGARIAN

Expressing yourself

pardon?
моля?
molya?

what?
какво?
kakvo?

could you repeat that, please?
бихте ли повторили, моля?
beehteh lee poftorili, molya?

could you speak more slowly?
може ли да говорите по-бавно?
mozheh lee da govoriteh po-bavno?

I don't understand
не разбирам
ne razbeeram

I understand a little Bulgarian
разбирам малко български
razbeeram malko bulgarski

I can understand Bulgarian but I can't speak it
разбирам български, но не мога да говоря
razbeeram bulgarski, no neh moga da govorya

I hardly speak any Bulgarian
почти не говоря български
pochtee neh govorya bulgarski

do you speak English?
говорите ли английски?
govoriteh lee angleeyski?

how do you say ... in Bulgarian
как се казва на български ...?
kak seh kazva na bulgarski ...?

how do you spell it?
как се пише?
kak seh peesheh?

what's that called in Bulgarian?
как се казва това на български?
kak seh kazva tova na bulgarski?

could you write it down for me?
моля, напишете ми го
molya, napisheteh mee go

Understanding

разбирате ли български?
razbeerateh lee bulgarski?
do you understand Bulgarian?

това е нещо като ...
tova eh neshto kato ...
it's a kind of ...

това значи ...
tova znachi ...
it means ...

ще ви го напиша
shteh vee go napeesha
I'll write it down for you

SPEAKING ABOUT THE LANGUAGE

Expressing yourself

I learned a few words from my phrasebook
научих няколко думи от моя разговорник
na-oochiH nyakolko doomi ot moya razgovornik

I can just about get by
оправям се
opravyam seh

I hardly know two words!
не знам и две думи!
neh znam ee dveh doomi!

I find Bulgarian a difficult language
мисля, че българският език е труден
meeslya, cheh bulgarskiyat ezeek eh trooden

I know the basics but no more than that
знам някои най-основни неща, но нищо повече
znam nyako-i nay-osnovni neshta, no neeshto povecheh

people speak too quickly for me
хората говорят много бързо за мене
Horata govoryat mnogo burzo za meneh

Understanding

говорите български много добре
govoriteh bulgarski mnogo dobreh
you speak very good Bulgarian

имате добро произношение
eemateh dobro pro-iznosheni-eh
you have a good accent

ASKING THE WAY

Expressing yourself

excuse me, can you tell me where the ... is, please?
извинете, моля, бихте ли ми казали къде е ...?
izvineteh, molya, beeHteh lee mee kazali kudeh eh ...?

which way is it to ...?
в коя посока е ...?
fko-ya posoka eh ...?

can you tell me how to get to ...?
можете ли да ми кажете как да стигна до ...?
mozheteh lee da mee kazheteh kak da steegna do ...?

is there a ... near here?
има ли ... наблизо?
eema lee ... nableezo?

could you show me on the map?
можете ли да ми покажете на картата?
mozheteh lee da mee pokazheteh na kartata?

is there a map of the town somewhere?
има ли някъде карта на града?
eema lee nyakudeh karta na graduh?

is it far?
далече ли е?
dalecheh lee eh?

I'm lost
загубих се
zagoobiH seh

I'm looking for ...
търся ...
tursya ...

Understanding

вървете след мен
vurveteh slet men
follow me

завийте
zaveeyteh
turn

качете се
kacheteh seh
go up

надясно
nadyasno
right

наляво
nalyavo
left

направо
napravo
straight ahead

продължете
produlzheteh
keep going

слезте
slesteh
go down

веднага след ъгъла е
vednaga slet ugula eh
it's just round the corner

завийте наляво при банката
zaveeyteh nalyavo pree bankata
turn left at the bank

завийте надясно на кръговото движение
zaveeyteh nadyasno na krugovoto dvizheni-eh
turn right at the roundabout

завийте по първото отклонение
zaveeyteh po purvoto otkloneni-eh
take the next exit

не е далече
neh eh dalecheh
it's not far

пеша ли сте?
pesha lee steh?
are you on foot?

първият *(m)*/**първата** *(f)*/**първото** *(n)* **отляво**
purvi-yat/purvata/purvoto otlyavo
it's the first/second/third on the left

с кола е на пет минути от тук
skola eh na pet minooti ot took
it's five minutes away by car

GETTING TO KNOW PEOPLE

The basics

bad лош *losh*
beautiful красив *kraseef*
boring скучен *skoochen*
cheap евтин *eftin*
expensive скъп *skup*
good добър *dobur*
great страхотен *straHoten*
interesting интересен *interesen*
nice хубав *Hoobaf*
not bad не лош *ne losh*
well добре *dobreh*
to hate мразя *mrazya*
to like харесвам *Haresvam*
to love обичам *obeecham*

INTRODUCING YOURSELF AND FINDING OUT ABOUT OTHER PEOPLE

Expressing yourself

my name's ...
казвам се ...
kazvam seh ...

how do you do!
приятно ми е
pri-yatno mee eh

this is my husband
това е мъжът ми
tova eh muzhut mee

what's your name?
как се казваш *(sg)*/казвате *(pl)*?
kak seh kazvash/kazvateh?

pleased to meet you!
приятно ми е
pri-yatno mee eh

this is my partner, Karen
това е приятелката ми Карен
tova eh pri-yatelkata mee karen

I'm English
аз съм англичанин *(m)*/англичанка *(f)*
as sum anglichanin/anglichanka

we're Welsh
ние сме от Уелс
nee-eh smeh ot oo-els

I'm from …
аз съм от …
as sum ot …

where are you from?
откъде сте?
otkudeh steh?

how old are you?
на колко години сте?
na kolko godeeni steh?

I'm 22
на двайсет и две
na dvayset ee dveh

what do you do for a living?
какво работите?
kakvo rabotiteh?

are you a student?
студент ли сте?
stoodent lee steh?

I work
работя
rabotya

I'm studying law
следвам право
sledvam pravo

I'm a teacher
учител *(m)*/учителка съм *(f)*
oocheetel/oocheetelka sum

I stay at home with the children
домакиня съм
domakeenya sum

I work part-time
работя на половин работен ден
rabotya na poloveen raboten den

I work in advertising
работя в рекламата
rabotya freklamata

I'm retired
пенсионер *(m)*/пенсионерка *(f)* съм
pensi-oner/pensi-onerka sum

I'm self-employed
имам фирма
eemam feerma

I have two children
имам две деца
eemam dveh detsa

we don't have any children
нямаме деца
nyamameh detsa

two boys and a girl
две момчета и едно момиче
dveh momcheta ee edno momeecheh

a boy of five and a girl of two
едно момче на пет години и едно момиче на две
edno momcheh na pet godeeni ee edno momeecheh na dveh

have you ever been to Britain?
Били ли сте във Великобритания?
bilee lee steh vuf velikobritaniya?

Understanding

Англичани ли сте?
anglichani lee steh?
are you English?

и ние сме на почивка тук
ee nee-eh smeh na pocheefka took
we're on holiday here too

много ми се иска да отида в Шотландия някой ден
mnogo mee seh eeska da oteeda fshotlandi-ya nyakoy den
I'd love to go to Scotland one day

Познавам Англия доста добре
poznavam angli-ya dosta dobreh
I know England quite well

TALKING ABOUT YOUR STAY

Expressing yourself

I'm here on business
тук съм по работа
took sum po rabota

we're on holiday
на почивка сме
na pocheefka smeh

I arrived three days ago
пристигнах преди три дни
pristeegnaH predee tree dnee

we've been here for a week
тук сме от една седмица
took smeh ot edna sedmitsa

I'm only here for a long weekend
тук съм само за почивните дни
took sum samo za pocheevnite dnee

we're just passing through
само минаваме оттук
samo minavameh ottook

this is our first time in Bulgaria
за първи път сме в България
za purvi put smeh v bulgari-ya

we're here to celebrate our wedding anniversary
тук сме да отпразнуваме годишнина от сватбата
took smeh da otpraznoovameh godeeshnina ot svadbata

we're on our honeymoon
на меден месец сме
na meden mesets smeh

we're here with friends
тук сме с приятели
took smeh spri-yateli

we're touring around
на екскурзия сме
na ekskoorzi-ya smeh

we managed to get a cheap flight
успяхме да намерим евтин полет
oospyaHmeh da namerim eftin polet

we're thinking about buying a house here
мислим да си купим къща тук
meeslim da see koopim kushta took

Understanding

за колко време сте тук?
za kolko vremeh steh took?
how long are you staying?

за първи път ли сте в България?
za purvi put lee steh v bulgari-ya?
is this your first time in Bulgaria?

Лриятно
pri-yatno iskarvaneh
enjoy your stay!

приятно изкарване до края на почивката
pri-yatno iskarvaneh do kraya na pocheefkata
enjoy the rest of your holiday!

харесва ли ви тук?
Haresva lee vee took?
do you like it here?

ходили ли сте в ...?
Hodili lee steh v ...?
have you been to ...?

STAYING IN TOUCH

Expressing yourself

we should stay in touch
трябва да си пишем
tryabva da see peeshem

I'll give you my e-mail address
ще ви дам имейл адреса си
shteh vee dam eemeyl adresa see

here's my address, in case you ever come to Britain
ето адресът ми, ако дойдете някога във Великобритания
eto adresut mee, ako doydeteh nyakoga vuf velikobritaniya

Understanding

вие сте винаги добре дошли у нас на гости
vee-eh steh veenagi dobreh doshlee oo nas na gosti
you're always welcome to come and stay with us here

имате ли имейл адрес?
eemateh lee eemeyl adres?
do you have an e-mail address?

ще ми дадете ли адреса си?
shteh mee dadeteh lee adresa see?
will you give me your address?

EXPRESSING YOUR OPINION

> **Some informal expressions**
> **горе-долу** *goreh-doloo* not bad, OK
> **кофти** *kofti* awful
> **супер** *sooper* great
> **много готино** *mnogo gotino* really great

Expressing yourself

I really like ...
... много ми харесва
... mnogo mee Haresva

I really liked ...
... много ми хареса
... mnogo mee Haresa

I don't like …
… не ми харесва
… neh mee Haresva

I didn't like …
… не ми хареса
… neh mee Haresa

I love …
обичам …
obeecham …

I loved …
… хареса ми
… Haresa mee

I would like …
бих искал *(m)*/искала *(f)* …
beeH eeskal/eeskala …

I would have liked …
искаше ми се …
eeskasheh mee seh …

I find it …
смятам, че е …
smyatam, cheh eh …

I found it …
смятам, че беше …
smyatam, cheh besheh …

it's lovely
прекрасно е
prekrasno eh

it was lovely
беше прекрасно
besheh prekrasno

I agree
съгласен *(m)*/съгласна *(f)* съм
suglasen/suglasna sum

I don't agree
не съм съгласен *(m)*/съгласна *(f)*
ne sum suglasen/suglasna

I don't know
не знам
neh znam

I don't mind
нямам нищо против
nyamam neeshto proteef

I don't like the sound of it
не ми звучи добре
neh mee zvoochee dobreh

it sounds interesting
звучи интересно
zvoochee interesno

it really annoys me
много ме нервира
mnogo meh nerveera

it was boring
беше скучно
besheh skoochno

it's a rip-off
това е пладнешки обир
tova eh pladneshki obir

it gets very busy at night
нощно време е претъпкано
noshtno vremeh eh pretupkano

it's too busy
много е претъпкано
mnogo eh pretupkano

it's very quiet
много е тихо
mnogo eh teeHo

I really enjoyed myself
беше ми много забавно
besheh mee mnogo zabavno

we had a great time
изкарахме чудесно
iskaraHmeh choodesno

there was a really good atmosphere
атмосферата беше много приятна
atmosferata besheh mnogo pri-yatna

we found a great hotel
намерихме чудесен хотел
nameriHmeh choodesen Hotel

we met some nice people
срещнахме много симпатични хора
sreshtnaHmeh mnogo simpateechni Hora

Understanding

много приятно място
mnogo pri-yatno myasto
it's a lovely area

не отивайте през уикенда, има много хора
neh oteevayteh prez oo-eekenda, eema mnogo Hora
don't go at the weekend, it's too busy

нищо особено
neeshto osobeno
it's a bit overrated

няма много туристи
nyama mnogo tooreesti
there aren't too many tourists

препоръчвам ви ...
preporuchvam vee ...
I recommend ...

приятно ли изкарахте?
pri-yatno lee iskaraHteh?
did you enjoy yourselves?

трябва да отидете в ...
tryabva da oteedeteh v...
you should go to ...

харесва ли ви ...?
Haresva lee vee ...?
do you like ...?

TALKING ABOUT THE WEATHER

Some informal expressions

вир вода съм *veer voda sum* I'm soaked *(with sweat or from the rain)*
измръзнах *izmruznaH* I'm freezing
страшна жега *strashna zhega* it's boiling
циганско лято *tseegansko lyato* Indian summer

Expressing yourself

have you seen the weather forecast for tomorrow?
знаете ли прогнозата за времето за утре?
zna-eteh lee prognozata za vremeto za ootreh?

it's going to be nice
времето ще бъде хубаво
vremeto shteh budeh Hoobavo

it isn't going to be nice
времето няма да бъде хубаво
vremeto nyama da budeh Hoobavo

it's really hot
много е горещо
mnogo eh goreshto

it gets cold at night
през нощта става студено
prez noshta stava stoodeno

the weather was beautiful
времето беше прекрасно
vremeto besheh prekrasno

it rained a few times
валя дъжд няколко пъти
valya dusht nyakolko puti

there was a thunderstorm
имаше гръмотевици
eemasheh grumotevitsi

it's very humid here
тук е много влажно
took eh mnogo vlazhno

it's been lovely all week
времето беше много приятно цялата седмица
vremeto besheh mnogo pri-yatno tsyalata sedmitsa

we've been lucky with the weather
имаме късмет с времето
eemameh kusmet svremeto

Understanding

облачно
слънчево

cloudy
sunny

очаква се да вали
ochakva seh da valee
it's supposed to rain

утре пак ще е горещо
ootreh pak shteh eh goreshto
it will be hot again tomorrow

прогнозата е за хубаво време до края на седмицата
prognozata eh za Hoobavo vremeh do kra-ya na sedmitsata
they've forecast good weather for the rest of the week

TRAVELLING

The basics

airport летище *leteeshteh*, аерогара *a-erogara*
boarding качване *kachvaneh*
boarding card бордна карта *bordna karta*
boat кораб(че) *korap(che)*
bus автобус *aftoboos*
bus station автогара *aftogara*
bus stop автобусна спирка *aftoboosna speerka*
car кола *kola*, автомобил *aftomobeel*
check-in регистрация *registratsi-ya*
coach автобус *aftoboos*
flight полет *polet*
gate изход *eesHot*
left-luggage (office) гардероб *garderop*
luggage багаж *bagash*
map карта *karta*
motorway магистрала *magistrala*
passport паспорт *pasport*
plane самолет *samolet*
platform перон *peron*
railway station (жепе) гара *(zhepe) gara*
return (ticket) (билет за) отиване и връщане *(bilet za) oteevaneh ee vrushtaneh*
road път *put*
single (ticket) еднопосочен (билет) *ednoposochen (bilet)*
street улица *oolitsa*
street map карта на града *karta na graduh*
taxi такси *taksee*
terminal терминал *terminal*
ticket билет *bilet*
timetable разписание *raspisani-eh*
town centre центъра на града *tsentura na graduh*
train влак *vlak*
tram трамвай *tramvay*
trolleybus тролей *troley*

underground метро *metro*
underground station станция на метрото *stantsi-ya na metroto*
to book запазвам, резервирам *zapazvam, rezerveeram*
to check in регистрирам се *registreeram se*
to hire наемам *na-emam*

Expressing yourself

where can I buy tickets?
къде мога да купя билети?
kudeh moga da koopya bileti?

a ticket to ..., please
един билет за ..., ако обичате
edeen bilet do ..., ako obeechateh

I'd like to book a ticket
искам да запазя билет
eeskam da zapazya bilet

how much is a ticket to ...?
колко струва един билет до ...?
kolko stroova edeen bilet do ...?

are there any concessions for students?
има ли намаление за студенти?
eema lee namaleni-eh za studenti?

could I have a timetable, please?
бихте ли ми дали едно разписание, моля?
beeHte lee mee dali edno raspisani-eh, molya?

is there an earlier/later one?
има ли ... по-рано/по-късно?
eema lee ... po-rano/po-kusno?

how long does the journey take?
за колко време се стига дотам?
za kolko vremeh seh steega dotam?

is this seat free?
мястото свободно ли е?
myastoto svobodno lee eh?

I'm sorry, there's someone sitting there
съжалявам, мястото е заето
suzhalyavam, myastoto eh za-eto

Understanding

анулиран	cancelled
билети	tickets
влизането забранено	no entry
връзка, връзки	connection(s)

всеки ден	every day
вход	entrance
жени	ladies
заминаващи	departures
изход	exit, gate
има закъснение	delayed
информация	information
мъже	gents
пристигащи	arrivals
отменен	cancelled
справки	inquiries
тоалетна	toilets

свободни места няма
svobodni mesta nyama
everything is fully booked

Making sense of abbreviations

жп (жепе) railway

БДЖ (Български Държавни Железници) Bulgarian National Railways

On timetables **кол.** stands for коловоз (track, platform) and **зак.** for закъснение (delay).

Days of the week may be abbreviated to: **пон., вт., ср., четв., пет., съб., нед.**

BY PLANE

Bulgaria's popularity is growing, and with it the number of airlines offering flights to the country. Besides regular scheduled flights between most European capitals and Sofia there are now direct flights from the UK to the Black Sea city of Varna. Some tour operators also offer charter flights to Bourgas, Varna and Plovdiv. Domestic flights serve the Sofia–Bourgas and Sofia–Varna routes, mainly during holiday periods (up to four flights a day from April to October).

Expressing yourself

where's the British Airways check-in?
къде е регистрацията за British Airways?
kudeh eh registratsi-yata za british airways?

I've got an e-ticket
моят билет е електронен
moyat bilet eh elektronen

what time do we board?
в колко часа да се качваме?
fkolko chasuh da seh kachvameh?

one suitcase and one piece of hand luggage
един куфар и една чанта ръчен багаж
edeen koofar ee edna chanta ruchen bagash

I'd like to confirm my return flight
искам да потвърдя полета за връщане
eeskam da potvurdyuh poleta za vrushtaneh

one of my suitcases is missing
един от куфарите ми липсва
edeen ot koofariteh mee leepsva

my luggage hasn't arrived
багажът ми не е пристигнал
bagazhut mee neh eh pristeegnal

the plane was two hours late
самолетът имаше два часа закъснение
samoletut eemasheh dva chasa zakusneni-eh

I've missed my connection
изпуснах връзката си
ispoosnaH vruskata see

I've left something on the plane
забравих нещо в самолета
zabraviH neshto fsamoleta

I want to report the loss of my luggage
искам да декларирам изгубен багаж
eeskam da deklareeram izgooben bagash

Understanding

без мито	duty free
вътрешни полети	domestic flights
зала (за) заминаващи	departure lounge
заминава	departs
кацнал	landed
качване незабавно	immediate boarding
митница	customs

нищо за деклариране	nothing to declare
паспортен контрол	passport control
получаване на багажа	baggage reclaim
предмети за деклариране	goods to declare
проверка	control
пристига	arrives
регистрация	check-in
свръхбагаж	overweight

багажът ви превишава лимита с пет килограма
bagazhut vee previshava limeeta spet kilograma
your luggage is five kilos overweight

до прозореца ли искате или до пътеката?
do prozoretsa lee eeskateh ilee do putekata?
would you like a window seat or an aisle seat?

ето бордната ви карта
eto bordnata vee karta
here's your boarding card

качването ще започне в ...
kachvaneto shteh zapochneh v ...
boarding will begin at ...

колко чанти имате?
kolko chanti eemateh?
how many bags do you have?

някой давал ли ви е нещо да носите в самолета?
nyakoy daval lee vee eh neshto da nositeh fsamoleta?
has anyone given you anything to take on board?

може да се обадите на този номер да проверите дали багажът ви е пристигнал
mozheh da seh obaditeh na tozi nomer da provereeteh dalee bagazhut vee eh pristeegnal
you can call this number to check if your luggage has arrived

моля, изчакайте в залата за заминаващи
molya, ischakayteh vzalata za zaminavashti
please wait in the departure lounge

моля, отправете се към изход номер ...
molya, otpraveteh se kum eesHot nomer ...
please proceed to gate number ...

сам *(m)*/**сама** *(f)* **ли сложихте багажа във всички чанти?**
sam/sama lee slozhiHteh bagazha vuf fseechki chanti?
did you pack all your bags yourself?

това е последно повикване за ...
tova eh posledno poveekvaneh za ...
this is a final call for ...

трябва да се прекачите в ...
tryabva da seh prekacheeteh v/vuf ...
you'll have to change in ...

BY TRAIN, COACH, BUS, UNDERGROUND, TRAM, TROLLEYBUS

Bulgaria's dense coach network provides inexpensive transport between towns. Every town has at least one coach station, with private companies providing modern, punctual buses to all the main destinations. Smaller places can generally be reached by public transport or local coach companies, whose vehicles tend to be more basic. The rail network is quite run-down but provides a reasonable service. The national rail company has a website featuring timetables and destinations in Bulgarian and English (**http://razpisanie.bdz.bg/**). Given the low prices, it can be worth buying a first-class ticket for long journeys. However, it's worth pointing out that coaches are generally faster.

Big cities have good public transport, and foreign visitors will find it very cheap. Tickets have to be bought in advance, either for one journey or for the day, and are on sale at most newspaper stands and at special booths around town. Be warned that stops are badly signposted and it's a good idea to get someone to confirm the names of the stops and the direction you're heading. Sofia has one underground line, which is very modern but serves an area with no real tourist attractions. Be careful not to confuse the buses, trams and trolleybuses in Sofia: they have the same numbers but do not all go in the same directions. Watch out for pickpockets on public transport! Taxis are cheap by Western European standards. Don't take a taxi parked immediately in front of a four- or five-star hotel but rather ask

reception to order you one. Always check the price list stuck on the front windscreen and side window of the taxi to make sure it has an acceptable price per kilometre, and keep an eye on the meter.

Expressing yourself

can I have a public transport map, please?
можете ли да ми дадете карта на градския транспорт, моля?
mozheteh lee da mee dadeteh karta na gratski-ya transport, molya?

what time is the next train to ...?
в колко часа е следващият влак за ...?
fkolko chasuh eh sledvashti-yat vlak za...?

what time is the last train?
в колко часа е последният влак за... ?
fkolko chasuh eh posledni-yat vlak za...?

which platform is it for ...?
на кой коловоз е влакът за ...?
na koy kolovos eh vlakut za ...?

where can I catch a bus to ...?
къде мога да хвана автобус за ...?
kudeh moga da Hvana aftoboos za ...?

which line do I take to get to ...?
кой номер да взема за ...?
koy nomer da vzema za ...?

is this the stop for ...?
това ли е спирката за ...?
tova lee eh speerkata za ...?

I've missed my train/bus
изпуснах влака си/автобуса си
ispoosnaH vlaka see/aftoboosa see

is this where the coach leaves for ...?
от тук ли тръгва автобусът за ...?
ot took lee trugva aftoboosut za ...?

can you tell me when I need to get off?
бихте ли ми казали кога да сляза?
beeHteh lee mee kazali koga da slyaza?

Understanding

билетен център	ticket office
билети за днес	tickets for travel today
бърз влак	express train

в двете посоки	in both directions
в работни дни	on week days
движи се сезонно	seasonal train
еднодневна карта	day pass
експрес	intercity train
климатик	air conditioning
коловоз	railway track
контрольор	ticket inspector
към влаковете	to the trains
месечна карта	monthly pass
метростанция	underground station
направление	destination
последна спирка	last stop
пътник, пътници	passenger(s)
пътнически влак	passenger train
резервации	bookings
рейс	bus/coach
седмична карта	weekly pass
сектор	bay
станция на метрото	underground station

влакът спира в ...
vlakut speera v/vuf ...
this train calls at ...

трябва да се прехвърлите в ...
tryabva da seh preHvurliteh v/vuf ...
you'll have to change at ...

има спирка малко по-надолу вдясно
eema speerka malko po-nadoloo vdyasno
there's a stop a bit further along on the right

на две спирки от тук
na dveh speerki ot took
two stops from here

само точни пари, моля
samo tochni paree, molya
exact money only, please

трябва да вземете автобус номер ...
tryabva da vzemeteh aftoboos nomer...
you need to get the number ... bus

BY CAR

Bulgaria is a small country and you can get around quite easily by car. Buy a road map before you set off, as signposting is not always clear and not all signs are written in Roman characters. Your home driving licence is valid in Bulgaria. There is a decent network of main roads, but smaller roads are often in very poor condition and are best avoided at night. When driving outside cities you must display a tax disc (**винетка** *vinetka*): this can be purchased at the border for a small fee. Police flag down cars randomly both within and outside of towns and cities: you should show your licence, the car's documents and insurance. They will also want to see your passport, which you should carry with you at all times. Your **талон** *talon*, a document which is marked by a police officer if you commit a driving offence, will only be relevant if you are permanently resident or have hired a car within the country. If you are stopped for a further offence, you will be fined. Hitchhiking is not recommended. There is a reasonable number of petrol stations, though it's best to use the big European companies. Be warned that thefts of foreign cars have become very common. Parking in all cities is a problem as there are not enough public car parks. In Sofia most of the city centre is "pay and display" with tickets being sold by patrolling ticket officers dressed in bright green vests. Don't risk parking on pavements or roadsides as your car may be towed away.

Expressing yourself

where can I find a service station?
къде има бензиностанция?
kudeh eema benzeenostantsi-ya?

lead-free petrol, please
безоловен бензин, моля
bezoloven benzeen, molya

how much is it per litre?
колко струва литърът?
kolko stroova leeturut?

we got stuck in a traffic jam
попаднахме на задръстване
popadnaHmeh na zadrustvaneh

is there a garage near here?
има ли сервиз наблизо?
eema lee servees nableezo?

can you help us to push the car?
можете ли да ни помогнете да бутнем колата?
mozheteh lee da nee pomogneteh da bootnem kolata?

the battery's dead
акумулаторът е паднал
akoomoolatorut eh padnal

I've broken down
колата ми се повреди
kolata mee seh povredee

we've run out of petrol
свърши ни бензинът
svurshi nee benzeenut

we've just had an accident
току-що катастрофирахме
tokoo-shto katastrofeeraHmeh

I've got a puncture and my spare tyre is flat
спуках гума, а резервната също е спукана
spookaH gooma, a rezervnata sushto eh spookana

I've lost my car keys
загубил *(m)*/загубила *(f)* съм ключовете на колата
zagoobil/zagoobila sum klyuchoveteh na kolata

how long will it take to repair?
за колко време ще я оправите?
za kolko vremeh shteh ya opraviteh?

◆ Hiring a car

I'd like to hire a car for a week
искам да наема кола за една седмица
eeskam da na-ema kola za edna sedmitsa

an automatic (car)
автоматична кола
aftomateechna kola

do I have to fill the tank up before I return it?
трябва ли да напълня резервоара преди да я върна?
tryabva lee da napulnya rezervo-ara predee da ya vurna?

I'd like to take out comprehensive insurance
искам да си направя пълна застраховка
eeskam da see napravya pulna zastraHofka

◆ Getting a taxi

I'd like to go to …
Искам да отида до …
eeskam da oteeda do …

is there a taxi rank near here?
има ли стоянка за такси наблизо?
eema lee stoyanka za taksee nableezo?

I'd like to book a taxi for 8pm
Искам да поръчам такси за 8 вечерта
eeskam da porucham taksee za osem vecherta

you can drop me off here, thanks
може да ме оставите тук, благодаря
mozheh da meh ostaviteh took, blagodaryuh

how much will it be to go to the airport?
колко ще ми струва до летището?
kolko shteh mee stroova do leteeshteto?

◆ Hitchhiking

I'm going to …
отивам в/във …
oteevam v/vuf …

could you take me as far as …?
можете ли да ме вземето до …?
mozheteh lee da meh vzemeteh do …?

we hitched a lift
взеха ни на автостоп
vzeHa nee na aftostop

can you drop me off here?
можете ли да ме оставите тук?
mozheteh lee da meh ostaviteh took?

Understanding

в обратна посока	in the opposite direction
злополука	accident
има свободни места	free spaces *(car park)*
коли под наем/rent-a-car	car hire
мини на долна предавка	switch to a lower gear
намали скоростта	slow down
няма свободни места	full *(car park)*
опасен завой	dangerous bend ahead
пазете талона	keep your ticket
паркинг	car park

паркирането забранено	no parking
пРестрой се	get in lane
пътят е в ремонт	road works ahead

покажете ми шофьорската си книжка
pokazheteh mee shofyorskata see kneeshka
I'll need your driving licence

трябва да оставите сто и петдесет евро депозит
tryabva da ostaviteh sto ee pedeset evro depozit
there's a €150 deposit

добре, влезте, ще ви закарам до ...
dobreh, vlezteh, shteh vee zakaram do ...
all right, get in, I'll take you as far as ...

BY BOAT

Boat services run between the Black Sea coastal towns. Cruises on the Danube are available, though it is no longer possible to cross the river to Romania as used to be the case.

Expressing yourself

I feel seasick
лошо ми е
losho mee eh

how long is the journey?
колко време трае пътуването?
kolko vremeh tra-eh putoovaneto?

Understanding

лодка	fishing boat
само за пешеходци	foot passengers only
следващият курс/рейс е в ...	next service at ...
яхта	yacht

TRAVELLING

ACCOMMODATION

Tourism is developing rapidly in Bulgaria and accommodation of all kinds is available throughout the country – from swish 4- and 5-star hotels through more cosy rural getaways – perhaps with mineral baths or organic farm food – down to very basic mountain huts. The **квартирно бюро** *kvart**eer**no byur**o*** in big cities and coastal tourist areas can give addresses of budget accommodation in private homes (advertised with English signs saying "room to rent"). You will usually have to share the family bathroom. For security reasons, it is now a legal requirement for hotels and private landlords to keep a guest register, and you will have to hand over some ID which will be returned to you when you leave. A new legal requirement means that foreigners and Bulgarians now pay the same prices. There should not be any additional tax. There are a few establishments similar to youth hostels (**туристическа спалня** *toorist**ee**cheska sp**a**lnya*) offering dormitories and shared washing facilities, but these are few and far between. The few campsites at the seaside have wonderful locations right on the beach, but the hygiene facilities leave something to be desired. Camping out in the open is illegal.

The basics

apartment апартамент *apartam**e**nt*
bath вана *v**a**na*
bathroom баня *b**a**nya*
bathroom with shower баня с душ *b**a**nya zdoosh*
bed легло *legl**o***
bed and breakfast нощувка и закуска *nosht**oo**fka ee zak**oo**ska*
cable television кабелна телевизия *k**a**belna telev**ee**zi-ya*
campsite къмпинг *k**u**mpink*
caravan каравана *karav**a**na*
cottage къща *k**u**shta*, вила *v**ee**la*
double bed двойно легло *dv**o**yno legl**o***
double room двойна стая *dv**o**yna st**a**-ya*
en-suite bathroom отделна баня *otd**e**lna b**a**nya*
family room семейна стая *sem**e**yna st**a**-ya*

flat апартамент *apartament*
full-board пълен пансион *pulen pansi-on*
fully inclusive цената включва всичко *tsenata fklyuchva fseechko*
half-board полупансион *poloo-pansi-on*
hotel хотел *Hotel*
key ключ *klyuch*
rent наем *na-em*
self-catering без храна *bes Hrana*
shower душ *doosh*
single bed единично легло *edineechno leglo*
single room единична стая *edineechna sta-ya*
tenant наемател *na-ematel*
tent палатка *palatka*
toilets тоалетни *to-aletna*
youth hostel туристическа спалня *tooristeecheska spalnya*
to book резервирам *rezeveeram*
to rent вземам под наем *vzemam pod na-em*
to reserve резервирам *rezerveeram*

Expressing yourself

I have a reservation
имам резервация
eemam rezervatsi-ya

the name's ...
името ми е ...
eemeto mee e...

do you take credit cards?
може ли да платя с кредитна карта?
mozheh lee da platyuh skreditna karta?

could you write the name down for me please?
може ли да ми напишете адреса?
mozheh lee da mee napeesheteh adresa?

Understanding

вход за външни лица забранен	staff only
няма свободни места	no vacancies
рецепция	reception
свободни легла/места	vacancies

стаи под наем	rooms to let
тоалетни	toilets
цена на човек	price per person
частен дом	private property

може ли да видя паспорта Ви, моля?
mozheh lee da veedya pasporta vee, molya?
could I see your passport, please?

попълнете тази бланка, ако обичате
populneteh tazi blanka, ako obeechateh
could you fill in this form?

HOTELS

Expressing yourself

do you have any vacancies?
имате ли свободни стаи?
eemateh lee svobodni sta-i?

how much is a double room per night?
колко струва една двойна стая на нощ?
kolko stroova edna dvoyna sta-ya na nosht?

I'd like to reserve a double room/a single room
искам да резервирам двойна/единична стая
eeskam da rezerveeram dvoyna/edineechna sta-ya

for three nights
за три нощи
za tree noshti

would it be possible to stay an extra night?
възможно ли е да остана още една нощ?
vuzmozhno lee e da ostana oshteh edna nosht?

do you have any rooms available for tonight?
имате ли свободни стаи за тази нощ?
eemateh lee svobodni sta-i za tazi nosht?

do you have any family rooms?
имате ли стаи за семейство?
eemateh lee sta-i za semeystvo?

would it be possible to add an extra bed?
може ли да донесете още едно легло?
mozheh lee da doneseteh oshteh edno leglo?

could I see the room first?
може ли първо да видя стаята?
mozheh lee purvo da veedya sta-yata?

I'd like to move to a different room, mine is too noisy
бих искал (m)/искала (f) да сменя стаята си, моята е много шумна
beeH eeskal/eeskala da smenyuh sta-yata see, mo-yata eh mnogo shoomna

do you have anything bigger/quieter?
имате ли нещо по-голямо/по-тихо?
eemateh lee neshto po-golyamo/po-teeHo?

that's fine, I'll take it
харесва ми, ще я взема
Haresva mee, shteh ya vzema

could you recommend any other hotels?
бихте ли ми препоръчали други хотели?
beeHteh lee mee preporuchali droogi Hoteli?

is breakfast included?
закуската включена ли е?
zakooskata fklyuchena lee eh?

what time do you serve breakfast?
в колко часа е закуската?
fkolko chasuh eh zakooskata?

is there a lift?
има ли асансьор?
eema lee asansyor?

what time will the room be ready?
кога ще бъде готова стаята?
koga shteh budeh gotova sta-yata?

is the hotel near the centre of town?
хотелът близо ли е до центъра на града?
Hotelut bleezo lee eh do tsentura na graduh?

the key for room ..., please
ключът за стая ..., ако обичате
klyuchut za sta-ya ..., ako obeechateh

could I have an extra blanket?
може ли да ми дадете още едно одеало?
mozheh lee da mee dadeteh oshteh edno ode-alo?

the air conditioning isn't working
климатикът не работи
klimateekut neh raboti

Understanding

за колко нощи сте?
za kolko noshti steh?
how many nights is it for?

закуската се сервира в ресторанта между седем и половина и девет
zakooskata seh serveera frestoranta mezhdoo sedem ee poloveena ee devet
breakfast is served in the restaurant between 7.30 and 9.00

имаме само една единична стая свободна
eemameh samo edna edineechna sta-ya svobodna
we only have a single room available

искате ли вестник сутринта?
eeskateh lee vesnik sootrinta?
would you like a newspaper in the morning?

как се казвате, моля?
kak seh kazvateh, molya?
what's your name, please?

може да оставите чантите си тук
mozheh da ostaviteh chantiteh see took
you can leave your bags here

ползвали ли сте минибара?
polzvali lee steh minibara?
have you used the minibar?

регистрирането започва на обяд
registreeraneto zapochva na obyat
check-in is from midday

стаята ви още не е готова
sta-yata vee oshteh neh eh gotova
your room isn't ready yet

съжалявам, но всичко е заето
suzhalyavam, no fseechko eh za-eto
I'm sorry, but we're full

трябва да напуснете преди единайсет сутринта
tryabva da napoosneteh predee edinayset sootrinta
you have to check out before 11am

YOUTH HOSTELS

Expressing yourself

do you have space for two people for tonight?
имате ли място за двама души за тази нощ?
eemateh lee myasto za dvama dooshi za tazi nosht?

we've booked two beds for three nights
резервирали сме две легла за три нощи
rezerveerali smeh dveh legla za tree noshti

could I leave my backpack at reception?
може ли да си оставя раницата на рецепцията?
mozheh lee da see ostavya ranitsata na retseptsi-yata?

do you have somewhere we could leave our bikes?
има ли къде да си оставим колелата?
eema lee kudeh da see ostavim kolelata?

I'll come back for it around 7 o'clock
ще се върна за него *(m/n)*/нея *(f)* към седем часа
shteh seh vurna za nego/neya kum sedem chasuh

there's no hot water
няма топла вода
nyama topla voda

the sink's blocked
умивалникът е запушен
oomivalnikut eh zapooshen

is there a shaver plug?
има ли контакт за самобръсначка?
eema lee kontakt za samobrusnachka?

Understanding

има чаршафи и възглавници
eema charshafi ee vuzglavnitsi
bed linen is provided

имате ли членска карта?
eemateh lee chlenska karta?
do you have a membership card?

туристическата спалня се отваря в шест вечерта
tooristeecheskata spalnya seh otvarya fshest vecherta
the hostel reopens at 6pm

SELF-CATERING

Expressing yourself

we're looking for somewhere to rent near a town
търсим да вземем нещо под наем близо до града
tursim da vzemem neshto pod na-em bleezo do graduh

where do we pick up/leave the keys?
откъде да вземем ключовете?/къде да оставим ключовете?
otkudeh da vzemem klyuchoveteh?/kudeh da ostavim klyuchoveteh?

is electricity included in the price?
електричеството включено ли е в цената?
elektreechestvoto fklyucheno lee eh ftsenata?

are bed linen and towels provided?
има ли чаршафи, възглавници и кърпи?
eema lee charshafi, vuzglavnitsi ee kurpi?

is a car necessary?
необходима ли е кола?
ne-opHodeema lee eh kola?

is there a pool?
има ли басейн?
eema lee baseyn?

is the accommodation suitable for elderly people?
квартирата удобна ли е за възрастни хора?
kvarteerata oodobna lee eh za vuzrasni Hora?

where is the nearest supermarket?
къде е най-близкият супермаркет?
kudeh eh nay-bleezki-yat soopermarket?

Understanding

всичко е включено в цената
fseechko eh fklyucheno ftsenata
everything is included in the price

къщата е напълно мебелирана
kushtata eh napulno mebeleerana
the house is fully furnished

моля, оставете къщата чиста и подредена след себе си
molya, ostaveteh kushtata cheesta ee podredena slet sebeh see
please leave the house clean and tidy after you leave

обща баня
opshta banya
shared bathroom facilities

ще имате нужда от кола в тази част на страната
shteh eemateh noozhda ot kola ftazi chast na stranata
you really need a car in this part of the country

CAMPING

Expressing yourself

is there a campsite near here?
има ли къмпинг наблизо?
eema lee kumpink nableezo?

I'd like to book a space for a two-person tent for three nights
искам да запазя място за двуместна палатка за три нощи
eeskam da zapazya myasto za dvoomestna palatka za tree noshti

how much is it a night?
колко струва на нощ?
kolko stroova na nosht?

where is the shower block?
къде са душовете?
kudeh sa dooshoveteh?

can we pay, please? we were at space ...
може ли да платим, моля? ние бяхме на място ...
mozheh lee da plateem, molya? nee-eh byaHmeh na myasto ...

Understanding

ако имате нужда от нещо, елате да попитате
ako eemateh noozhda ot neshto, elateh da popeetateh
if you need anything, just come and ask

обадете ми се, ако имате някакви проблеми
obadeteh mee seh, ako eemateh nyakakvi problemi
let me know if you have any problems

струва ... лева на нощ за един човек
stroova ... leva na nosht za edeen chovek
it's ... per person per night

You can eat and drink in restaurants (**ресторант** *restorant*), taverns (**механа** *mehana*), coffee shops (**сладкарница** *slatkarnitsa*) and cafes (**кафене** *kafeneh*). Most places serve food until 10 or 11pm. All should have specific smoking and non-smoking areas but in reality implementation is patchy.

If you order bread with your meal you will have a choice of sliced bread (**на филии** *na filee-i*) or rolls (**питка** *peetka*). If you order water you will usually be served bottled local mineral water (**минерална вода** *mineralna voda*).

For freshly squeezed juice ask for **фреш** *fresh*; the phrase **натурален сок** *natooralen sok* actually means bottled fruit juice. Coffee is more popular than tea and is generally a very strong espresso. To get a weaker espresso you can order a "long" one (**дълго** *dulgo*), with more water, or you can ask if they have filter coffee (**шварцкафе** *shvartskafeh*). If you want it white then ask for coffee creamer (**сметана** *smetana*).

To order tea (**чай** *chay*), you must specify whether you want **черен чай** *cheren chay* (black tea) or **зелен чай** *zelen chay* (green tea). Otherwise you will probably get herbal tea: **билков чай** *beelkof chay* is tea made from herbs and **плодов чай** *plodof chay* is made from dried fruits. These are frequently drunk with honey (**мед** *met*) which you should order separately. The most common alcoholic drinks are **ракия** *rakee-ya* (a liqueur made from plums, grapes or other fruit), vodka, gin, whisky, wine (local wine is very good) and beer (usually lager). It is common to have a glass of *rakee-ya* before a meal with a salad starter and move on to wine for the main course. People don't usually drink without nibbling something – even if you're just having a glass of wine, it's customary to order a little snack like a bit of cheese (**сирене** *seereneh*) or nuts (**ядки** *yatki*). The legal drinking age in Bulgaria is 18.

Tipping is expected if you are satisfied with the service; 10% is a good rule to go by but check to make sure it hasn't already been added to the bill.

The basics

beer бира *beera*
bill сметка *smetka*
black coffee кафе без мляко *kafeh bes mlyako*
bottle бутилка *booteelka*
bread хляб *Hlyap*
breakfast закуска *zakooska*
coffee кафе *kafeh*
Coke® кола *kola*
dessert десерт *desert*
dinner вечеря *vecherya*
fruit juice плодов сок *plodof sok*
lemonade лимонада *limonada*
lunch обяд *obyat*
main course основно ястие *osnovno yasti-eh*
menu меню *menyu*
mineral water минерална вода *mineralna voda*
red wine червено вино *cherveno veeno*
rosé wine вино розе *veeno rozeh*
salad салата *salata*
sandwich сандвич *sandvich*
service обслужване *opsloozhvaneh*
sparkling *(water, wine)* газиран *gazeeran*
starter ордьовър *ordyovur*
still *(water)* негазирана *negazeerana*
tea чай *chay*
tip бакшиш *baksheesh*
water вода *voda*
white coffee кафе с мляко *kafeh smlyako*
white wine бяло вино *byalo veeno*
wine вино *veeno*
wine list менюто с вината *menyuto svinata*
to eat ям *yam*
to have breakfast закусвам *zakoosvam*
to have dinner вечерям *vecheryam*
to have lunch обядвам *obyadvam*
to order поръчвам *poruchvam*

Expressing yourself

shall we go and have something to eat?
да отидем ли да хапнем нещо?
da oteedem lee da Hapnem neshto?

do you want to go for a drink?
искаш *(sg)*/искате *(pl)* ли да отидем да пийнем нещо?
eeshkash/eeskateh lee da oteedem da peeynem neshto?

can you recommend a good restaurant?
можете ли да препоръчате добър ресторант?
mozheteh lee da preporuchateh dobur restorant?

excuse me! *(to call the waiter)*
може ли?
mozheh lee?

cheers!
наздраве!
nazdraveh!

that was lovely
беше много вкусно
besheh mnogo fkoosno

where are the toilets, please?
извинете, къде е тоалетната?
izvineteh, kudeh eh to-aletnata?

could you bring us an ashtray, please?
един пепелник, моля?
edeen pepelneek, molya?

EATING AND DRINKING

Understanding

храна за вкъщи   takeaway

съжалявам, не приемаме поръчки след 11 вечерта
suzhalyavam, neh pri-emameh poruchki slet edinayset vecherta
I'm sorry, we stop serving at 11pm

RESERVING A TABLE

Expressing yourself

I'd like to reserve a table for tomorrow evening
искам да запазя маса за утре вечерта
eeskam da zapazya masa za ootreh vecherta

for two people
за двама
za dvama

around 8 o'clock
около осем часа
okolo osem chasuh

do you have a table available any earlier than that?
имате ли свободна маса за по-рано?
eemateh lee svobodna masa za po-rano?

I've reserved a table – the name's ...
имам запазена маса, казвам се ...
eemam zapazena masa, kazvam se ...

Understanding

запазена
reserved

за колко часа?
za kolko chasuh?
for what time?

за колко души/човека?
za kolko dooshi/choveka?
for how many people?

как се казвате?
kak se kazvateh?
what's the name?

за пушачи или непушачи?
za pooshachi ilee nepooshachi?
smoking or non-smoking?

имате ли резервация?
eemateh lee rezervatsi-ya?
do you have a reservation?

тази маса в ъгъла харесва ли ви?
tazi masa fugula Haresva lee vee?
is this table in the corner OK for you?

съжалявам, но няма места в момента
suzhalyavam, no nyama mesta fmomenta
I'm afraid we're full at the moment

ORDERING FOOD

Expressing yourself

yes, we're ready to order
да, готови сме с поръчката
da, gotovi smeh sporuchkata

no, could you give us a few more minutes?
не, дайте ни още няколко минути, ако обичате
ne, dayteh nee oshteh nyakolko minooti, ako obeechateh

I'd like …
искам …
eeskam …

could I have …?
може ли …?
mozheh lee …?

I'm not sure, what's "чушка бюрек"?
не съм сигурен (m)/сигурна (f), какво е чушка бюрек?
ne sum seegooren/seegurna, kakvo eh chooshka byurek?

I'll have that
ще взема това
shteh vzema tova

I'm allergic to nuts/wheat/seafood/citrus fruit
алергичен (m)/алергична (f) съм към ядки/жито/морски
специалитети/цитрусови плодове
alergeechen/alergeechna sum kum yatki/zheeto/morski spetsi-aliteti/tseetrusovi plodoveh

does it come with vegetables?
с гарнитура от зеленчуци ли е?
zgarnitoora ot zelenchootsi lee eh?

what are today's specials?
какви са специалитетите за днес?
kakvee sa spetsi-alitetiteh za dnes?

what desserts do you have?
какви десерти имате?
kakvee deserti eemateh?

some water, please
малко вода, ако обичате
malko voda, ako obeechateh

that's for me
това е за мене
tova eh za meneh

a bottle of red/white wine
една бутилка червено/бяло вино
edna booteelka cherveno/byalo veeno

this isn't what I ordered, I wanted …
аз не поръчах това, аз исках …
az neh poruchaH tova, as eeskaH …

could we have some more bread, please?
още малко хляб, ако обичате
oshteh malko Hlyap, ako obeechateh

could you bring us another jug of water, please?
бихте ли донесли още една кана вода, моля?
beehteh lee donesli oshteh edna kana voda, molya?

Understanding

готови ли сте с поръчката?
gotovi lee steh sporuchkata?
are you ready to order?

съжалявам, ... свърши
suzhalyavam, ... svurshi
I'm sorry, we don't have any ... left

желаете ли десерт или кафе?
zhela-eteh lee desert ilee kafeh?
would you like dessert or coffee?

ще дойда след няколко минути
shteh doyda slet nyakolko minooti
I'll come back in a few minutes

какво ще желаете за пиене?
kakvo shteh zhela-eteh za pee-eneh?
what would you like to drink?

хареса ли ви?
Haresa lee vee?
was everything OK?

BARS AND CAFÉS

Expressing yourself

I'd like ...
искам ...
eeskam ...

a glass of white/red wine
една чаша бяло/червено вино
edna chasha byalo/cherveno veeno

a cup of tea
една чаша чай
edna chasha chay

a cup of hot chocolate
една чаша топъл шоколад
edna chasha topul shokolat

a Coke®/a diet Coke®
кола/кола лайт
kola/kola layt

a black/white coffee
едно кафе/кафе с мляко
edno kafeh/kafeh smlyako

a coffee and a croissant
едно кафе и един кроасан
edno kafeh ee edeen kro-asan

the same again, please
още веднъж същото, моля
oshteh vednush sushtoto, molya

Understanding

безалкохолно
напитки

какво ще обичате?
kakvo shteh obeechateh?
what would you like?

non-alcoholic
drinks

това е зоната за непушачи
tova eh zonata za nepooshachi
this is the non-smoking area

50

може ли да платите веднага, моля?
mozheh lee da plateeteh vednaga, molya?
could I ask you to pay now, please?

с лед/с лимон ли?
slet/slimon lee?
would you like ice/lemon with it?

Some informal expressions

преядох *preyadoH* I ate too much
махмурлия съм *maHmoorlee-ya sum* I have a hangover
прекалих с пиенето *prekaleeH spee-eneto* I had too much to drink
кръчма *kruchma* pub

THE BILL

Expressing yourself

the bill, please
сметката, моля
smetkata, molya

do you take credit cards?
приемате ли кредитни карти?
pri-emateh lee kreditni karti?

is service included?
в сметката има ли включен сервиз?
fsmetkata eema lee fklyuchen servees?

how much do I owe you?
колко ви дължа?
kolko vee dulzhuh?

I think there's a mistake in the bill
мисля, че има грешка в сметката
meeslya, cheh eema greshka fsmetkata

Understanding

всички заедно ли плащате?
fseechki za-edno lee plashtateh?
are you all paying together?

да, сервизът е включен в сметката
da, serveezut eh fklyuchen fsmetkata
yes, service is included

FOOD AND DRINK

Many first-time visitors are unaware of the range of culinary delights on offer in Bulgaria, including lovely fresh vegetables and fruit, and rich dishes flavoured with all kinds of herbs and spices. The cooking style tends to favour either grilled/barbecued meats or stew-type dishes cooked for hours on a low heat. Meat and two veg is not the usual format for a meal. The staple here is bread, eaten not just with a starter or soup but also frequently to accompany the main course. Dishes tend to be served as and when they are ready, so it may be useful to stipulate when you would like which course so that one person doesn't get all their food at once while another sits with an empty plate in front of them.

аламинути quick dishes
блюдо dish
в пещ in a wood-burning oven
варен boiled
вегетариански vegetarian
гарнитура side order
горещ hot
гърне clay pot
гювече individual clay pot
домашен home-made
задушен braised
каничка ... a pot of ...
лют(ив) very hot *(spicy)*
на грил grilled
на жар on coals
на керемида on a tile
на пара steamed
на скара barbecued
паниран battered

печен baked, roast
пикантен spicy
плато от ... a selection of/platter of ...
поднесен със served with
постен meat-free
пресен fresh
пушен smoked
пържен fried
сач large clay plate on which food is served still cooking
сос sauce
специалитет speciality
студен cold
суров raw
сушен dried
топъл warm
хрупкав crunchy
ястие meal

◆ salads салати

The salad is an obligatory start to any meal in Bulgaria, and it's a great way to partake of the wonderful seasonal vegetables. Salads are usually accompanied by a glass of the local spirit **ракия** *rakee-ya*. In winter when the vegetables lose their taste, people tend to eat less fresh salad and more home pickled vegetables, known as **туршия** *toorshee-ya*. The quintessential Bulgarian salad is **шопска салата** *shopska salata*, a delicious mixture of chopped tomatoes, cucumbers and roast peppers, topped with **сирене** *seereneh*, a feta-style cheese.

зелена салата lettuce, green salad
зелена салата с яйце green salad with boiled egg
зелена салата с риба тон green salad with tuna
картофена салата potato salad
кисели краставици pickled gherkins
кьополу puree of roast aubergine, garlic and peppers
лютеница puree of roast peppers, tomatoes and garlic
люти чушки chilli peppers
мешана салата mixed salad (usually chopped tomatoes and cucumbers)
печени чушки с доматен сос roast peppers with tomato sauce
руска салата Russian salad (chopped ham, potatoes and peas in mayonnaise dressing)
салата домати и краставици (sliced) tomato and cucumber salad
салата зеле и моркови grated salad of cabbage and carrots
салата зеле и моркови с майонеза coleslaw
снежанка salad of thick yogurt and either fresh or pickled cucumbers
туршия salad of pickled vegetables
шопска салата shopska salad *(see information panel above)*

◆ starters предястия

гъби в масло mushrooms cooked in butter
гъши дроб goose liver
домашна наденица home-made sausage
картофени кюфтета potato rissoles
кашкавал пане breaded kashkaval (yellow cheese)

FOOD AND DRINK

мишмаш mishmash (scrambled eggs with tomatoes, cheese and roast peppers)

мозък пане breaded brain

омлет натюр plain omelette

омлет със сирене/с гъби/с шунка/с кашкавал omelette with white cheese/mushrooms/ham/yellow cheese

пилешки сърчица chicken hearts

плато от колбаси platter of dried meats

постни сърми vine leaves stuffed with rice

пълнени чушки stuffed peppers

пържени тиквички със сос от кисело мляко fried strips of courgette with yogurt sauce

сирене по шопски white cheese cooked in butter in a clay pot with an egg on top

спаначени кюфтета spinach burgers

сърми с кайма vine leaves or sauerkraut leaves stuffed with minced meat

чушка бюрек breaded pepper stuffed with cheese

чушки пълнени с кайма peppers stuffed with minced meat

чушки пълнени със сирене и яйце peppers stuffed with cheese and eggs

чушки пълнени с ориз peppers stuffed with rice

пастърма pastrami

◆ soups супи

боб чорба bean soup

кремсупа от картофи/моркови/гъби cream of potato/carrot/mushroom soup

курбан koorban (meat and vegetable soup, originally prepared as a ritual offering)

леща lentil soup

пилешка супа chicken soup

пролетна супа spring vegetable soup

спаначена супа spinach soup

супа топчета meatball soup

телешко варено chunky beef and vegetable soup

таратор chilled yogurt and cucumber soup

шкембе чорба tripe soup, served with a strong garlic and vinager sauce

◆ snacks закуски

Traditional snacks such as **баница** *banitsa* and **боза** *boza* (a fermented wheat drink) are being edged out by foreign inventions such as pizza and doner kebabs. In spring and summer you will see boiled corn on the cob on sale everywhere on the streets. In the autumn roast chestnuts are the order of the day. You may see a lot of people eating toasted sunflower seeds and spitting out the black shells.

айран refreshing drink of watered-down yogurt flavoured with salt
баница (със сирене/с праз/с тиква) banitsa (layers of flaky pastry with cheese/leek/pumpkin)
баница бюрек banitsa with cheese and egg filling
варена/сладка царевица boiled (whole) corn on the cob
геврек small ring of bread, similar to a bagel
дюнер doner kebab
качамак polenta cooked with butter and topped with feta-style cheese
кебапче hand-rolled grilled sausage
кифла sweet bread roll filled with jam
козунак sweet Easter bread
кюфте hand-made grilled burger
мезе mezze, snack to accompany drinks
печена тиква baked pumpkin
печени кестени roast chestnuts
питка flat bread cooked on the bottom of the oven
пица на парче slice of pizza
погача large round loaf of bread prepared on special occasions
принцеса minced meat on toast
пуканки popcorn
пържени картофи french fries
сандвич sandwich
сладолед ice cream
слънчогледови семки sunflower seeds
тиквени семки pumpkin seeds
тост toasted sandwich
хот дог hot dog

◆ main courses основно ястие

Main courses are usually meat based. Vegetarians will fare best if they are here during the fasting periods in the run-up to Easter and Christmas; otherwise they tend to be offered meals with the two basic types of cheese, both unfamiliar to British tastes: **сирене** see*reneh* is similar to feta while **кашкавал** *kashkaval*, also frequently referred to as "yellow cheese", is a slightly rubbery variety. Both types of cheese can be made from either cow's or sheep's milk.

The meat of choice tends to be lamb, chicken or pork and more rarely beef. You can also find game (**дивеч** *deevech*) on offer. Duck and goose are also popular.

агнешки котлет lamb cutlet
агнешко печено roast lamb
агнешко по гергьовденски Gergyovden lamb (whole baked lamb with stuffing made of rice and innards)
болярско кюфте large hand-rolled burger with a filling, usually cheese
гювеч meat and vegetable stew
дроб сърма rice and liver dish
каре (свинско/телешко) steak (pork/beef)
кърначе round sausage
мусака moussaka
нервозни кюфтета "nervous" (ie very spicy) burgers
пуйка със зеле turkey cooked with pickled cabbage
пържола (пилешка/свинска) pork/chicken chop
свински джолан pork knuckle
свинско със зеле pork cooked with pickled cabbage
филе от елен по ловджийски hunter-style venison fillet
чеверме meat (lamb, goat or pig) cooked on the spit, usually served with a stuffing of rice and innards
шашлик large skewer of barbecued meat
шишче (пилешко/свинско) small skewer (chicken/pork)
шницел по виенски wiener schnitzel

◆ meat-free dishes постни ястия

боб яхния bean stew
задушени зеленчуци braised vegetables
зеле на фурна oven-baked cabbage
зелен фасул плакия green bean stew, cooked in the oven with lots of onions
постен гювеч vegetable stew
тиквички с ориз courgettes with rice, baked in the oven

◆ fish риба

The choice of fish is not wide, with several freshwater fish on offer from Bulgaria's rivers and a few fish from the Black Sea (mullet, turbot and some local species). Fresh fish imported from Greece can be found at upmarket restaurants.

бяла риба пане white fish, usually cod, in batter
калкан turbot
кефал mullet
лаврак sea bass, imported from Greece
миди с вино mussels in wine
попче goby, the most common fish around the Black Sea
пъстърва trout
пържена акула fried shark
пържена пъстърва fried trout
пъстърва на скара grilled trout
раци prawns
речни раци freshwater crayfish
риба меч на грил grilled swordfish
сафрид horse mackerel, a small Black Sea fish usually served fried
скариди shrimps
скумрия на скара grilled mackerel
сом catfish
сьомга със сос бешамел salmon with béchamel sauce
шаран в доматен сос carp in tomato sauce
шаран плакия carp cooked in the oven with lots of onions
хайвер fish roe

FOOD AND DRINK

57

черен/червен хайвер black/red caviar
черноморски ... Black Sea ...
ципура sea bream, imported from Greece

◆ desserts сладкиш/десерт

Bulgaria is not known for its desserts. The best choice of sweet things is usually to be found in cake shops.

баклава baklava
биволско кисело мляко buffalo yogurt
гараш торта a popular chocolate cake
грис халва cold semolina pudding, often with jellied fruits or raisins inside
кекс cake
кисело мляко със сладко от боровинки yogurt with blueberry jam
крем карамел crème caramel
крем брюле crème brûlée
млечна баница a sweet pastry dessert
овче кисело мляко sheep's milk yogurt
палачинка с мед и орехи/с шоколад/със сладко pancake with honey and walnuts/with chocolate spread/with jam
торта cream cake
щрудел strudel (usually apple)

FOOD AND DRINK GLOSSARY

агнешко lamb
айран/айрян yogurt drink
акула shark
ананас pineapple
бадем almond
бамя okra
банан banana
безкофеиново кафе decaffeinated coffee
биволско сирене buffalo-milk cheese
билков чай herbal tea
бира beer
бисквита biscuit
бифтек beef steak (can be made from minced meat)

боб beans
бонфиле fillet
боровинка blueberry
босилек basil
брашно flour
броколи broccoli
брюкселско зеле Brussels sprout
бульон thin soup
бъбреци kidney
бъркани яйца scrambled eggs
варено яйце boiled egg
вино wine
вишна sour cherry
газирана напитка fizzy drink
горски плодове berries

горчица mustard
грах peas
греяна ракия hot *rakee-ya (local spirit)*
грозде grape
гроздова ракия grape *rakee-ya (local spirit)*
гъба mushroom
гъска goose
дафинов лист bay leaf
див чесън wild garlic
дива ягода wild strawberry
диня watermelon
домат tomatoes
доматен сок tomato juice
дроб liver
дюла quince
език tongue
еспресо espresso
заек rabbit
заквасена сметана soured cream
закуска breakfast
захар sugar
зеле cabbage
зелен боб green beans
зелен чай green tea
зелена салата lettuce
зеленчук vegetable
зехтин olive oil
зърнени храни grains, cereals
кайма mince
кайсия apricot
каламари fried squid
картоф potato
картофено пюре mashed potatoes
катък type of cottage cheese
кафе coffee
кашкавал cheese
кашу cashew nut
киви kiwi
кисели краставици pickled gherkin
кисело зеле pickled cabbage *(similar to sauerkraut)*
кисело мляко yogurt
козе сирене goat's cheese
конфитюр jam
коняк brandy
копър dill
кори flaky pastry, filo pastry

краставица cucumber
кремвирш frankfurter sausage
круша pear
кълнове beansprouts
лаврак sea bream
лешник hazelnut
лимон lemon
локум Turkish delight
лук onion
луканка dried spicy sausage
магданоз parsley
майонеза mayonnaise
макарони pasta
маково семе poppy seeds
малина raspberry
манатарка porcini mushrooms
мандарина satsuma
маргарин margarine
мармелад smooth jam (with no bits)
маруля lettuce
маслина olive
масло butter
мед honey
мента/джоджан mint
месо meat
минерална вода mineral water
млечни продукти dairy products
мозък brain
морков carrot
напитка drink
натурален шоколад plain chocolate
нискомаслено low-fat
нискомаслено мляко skimmed milk
обяд lunch
овесени ядки porridge oats
овче сирене sheep's-milk cheese
олио oil (usually sunflower)
орех walnut
оцет vinegar
палачинка pancake
пастет pâté
патица duck
патладжан aubergine
пелин white wine with added bitter herbs
печурка button mushroom
пилешки гърди chicken breast
пилешки дробчета chicken livers
пилешки крилца chicken wings

пилешко chicken
пилешко бутче chicken leg
пипер pepper
питка bread roll
плод fruit
плодов чай fruit tea
подправки/билки herbs
портокал orange
портокалов сок orange juice
праз лук leeks
праскова peach
препечен хляб toast
пресен лук spring onion
пресни зеленчуци raw vegetables
прясно мляко milk
птиче месо poultry
пудра захар powdered sugar
пуйка turkey
пушена сьомга smoked salmon
пъдпъдъчи яйца quail's eggs
пъпеш melon
пържени яйца fried eggs
пъстърва trout
пюре puree
ребра ribs
репичка radish
риба fish
риба тон tuna
риган oregano
рохко яйце soft-boiled egg
рукола rocket
ръжен хляб rye bread
ряпа turnip
салам salami
свинско pork
синьо сирене blue cheese
сирене cheese
сирене крема cream cheese
скарида shrimp
сладки biscuits
сладко jam
сладолед ice cream
слива plum
сливова ракия plum *rakee-ya (local spirit)*
сметана cream
смокиня fig
соево сирене tofu

сок juice
сок от грейпфрут grapefruit juice
сол salt
спагети pasta
спанак spinach
стафида raisin
стек steak
субпродукти offal
суджук horseshoe-shaped dried sausage (made of beef with spices)
сърце heart
твърдо сварено яйце hard-boiled egg
телешко beef
тесто pastry
тиква pumpkin
тиквичка courgette
топено сирене processed cheese
торта cake
филе fillet
франзела baguette
фреш freshly squeezed juice
фурма date
фъстък peanut
хлебче bread roll
хляб bread
царевица corn
цаца whitebait
целина celery
ципура sea bass
червено вино red wine
червено цвекло beetroot
черен пипер black pepper
черен хляб brown bread
череша cherry
чесън garlic
чешмяна вода tap water
чубрица summer savoury
чушка pepper
шаран carp
шейк milk shake
шницел schnitzel
шоколад chocolate
шунка ham
ябълка apple
ябълков сок apple juice
ягода strawberry
ядки nuts

GOING OUT

There are free English-language guides and an English-language newspaper in Sofia with detailed info on local entertainment. In other towns and cities Bulgarian-language entertainment guides are available free in hotels, restaurants, cafes, bars, shops and cinemas and the information is listed in such a way that it should be easy to comprehend. You will find the prices for opera, concerts and other arts events very reasonable and the quality is high. Most cities now have modern multiplex cinemas with several screens. Cinema-going is still good value for money and most films are shown in the original language with Bulgarian subtitles.

You can hear typically Balkan music (**чалга** *chalga*) in cafés, on the radio and in nightclubs, where dancing on the tables is not uncommon.

People generally go out around 8pm and may stay out until the small hours, though in cities it is also customary to go for a drink after work and go home around 8pm. Almost all bars, cafes and clubs have waiter service and you pay the bill when you leave – often the bill for the whole table will be combined, so if you expressly want your own bill you should make this clear to the waiter at the beginning.

Bulgarians also like to entertain at home. If you are invited to someone's house (**отивам на гости** *oteevam na gosti*), you should be on time and bring something to drink, as well as some flowers for the lady of the house, if there is one. Don't be surprised if your hostess spends most of the evening in the kitchen and makes a tremendous fuss of you.

The basics

ballet балет *balet*
band оркестър *orkestur*, група *groopa*
bar бар *bar*
celebration празненство *praznenstvo*
cinema кино *keeno*
circus цирк *tseerk*
classical music класическа музика *klaseecheska moozika*

club клуб *kloop*
concert концерт *kontsert*
dubbed film дублиран филм *doobleeran film*
festival фестивал *festival*
film филм *feelm*
folk music народна музика *narodna moozika*
group група *groopa*
modern dance съвременни танци *suvremenni tantsi*
musical музикален *moozikalen*
opera опера *opera*
party събиране *subeeraneh*, парти *parti*
play пиеса *pi-esa*
pop music поп музика *pop moozika*
rock music рок *rok*
show шоу *sho-oo*
subtitled film филм със субтитри *film sus soopteetri*
theatre театър *te-atur*
ticket билет *bilet*
to book запазвам *zapazvam*
to go out излизам *izleezam*

SUGGESTIONS AND INVITATIONS

Expressing yourself

where can we go?
къде можем да отидем?
kudeh mozhem da oteedem?

what do you want to do?
какво ти *(sg)*/ви *(pl)* се прави?
kakvo tee/vee seh pravi?

I'd love to
с удоволствие
soodovolstvi-eh

shall we go for a drink?
да отидем ли да пийнем нещо?
da oteedem lee da peeynem neshto?

what are you doing tonight?
какво ще правиш *(sg)*/правите *(pl)* довечера?
kakvo shteh pravish/praviteh dovechera?

do you have plans?
имаш *(sg)*/имате *(pl)* ли планове?
eemash/eemateh lee planoveh?

I'm not sure I can make it
не знам дали ще успея
neh znam dalee shteh oospe-ya

would you like to ...?
искате ли да ...?
*ee*skateh lee da ...?

we were thinking of going to ...
мислим да отидем на ...
*mee*slim da ot*ee*dem na ...

I can't today, but maybe some other time
днес не мога, но някой друг път, може би
dnes neh moga, no nyakoy drook put, mozheh bee

ARRANGING TO MEET

Expressing yourself

what time shall we meet?
кога да се срещнем?
koga da seh sreshnem?

where shall we meet?
къде да се срещнем?
kudeh da seh sreshnem?

would it be possible to meet a bit later?
може ли да се срещнем малко по-късно?
mozheh lee da seh sreshnem malko po-kusno?

I have to meet ... at nine
имам среща с ... в девет часа
eemam sreshta s ... vdevet chasuh

see you tomorrow night
ще се видим утре вечер
shteh seh veedim ootreh vecher

I don't know where it is but I'll find it on the map
не знам къде е, но ще го намеря на картата
ne znam kudeh eh, no shteh go namerya na kartata

I'll meet you later, I have to stop by the hotel first
ще се видим по-късно, първо трябва да мина през хотела
shteh seh veedim po-kusno, purvo tryabva da meena pres Hotela

I'll call/text you if there's a change of plan
ако има промяна в плановете, ще ти звънна/пратя есемес
ako eema promyana fplanoveteh, shteh tee zvunna/pratya esemes

sorry I'm late
извинете за закъснението
izvineteh za zakusneni-eto

Understanding

аз черпя
as cherpya
it's my treat/my round

да вдигнем тост
da vdeegnem tost
let's make a toast

можем да се срещнем пред ... **това устройва ли те** *(sg)***/ви** *(pl)***?**
mozhem da seh sreshnem pret ... *tova oostroyva lee teh/vee?*
we can meet outside ... is that OK with you?

ще дойда да те *(sg)***/ви** *(pl)* **взема към осем**
shteh doyda da teh/vee vzema kum osem
I'll come and pick you up about 8 o'clock

ще се видим там
shteh seh veedim tam
I'll meet you there

ще ти дам телефона си и може утре да ми се обадиш
shteh tee dam telefona see ee mozheh ootreh da mee seh obadish
I'll give you my number and you can call me tomorrow

Some informal expressions

да хапнем *da Hapnem* to have a bite to eat
по една чашка *po edna chashka* a quick drink
купон *koopon* party
да изпия на екс *da ispee-ya na eks* to drink it down in one

FILMS, SHOWS AND CONCERTS

Expressing yourself

is there a guide to what's on?
има ли програма на кината и театрите?
eema lee programa na kinata ee te-atriteh?

I'd like three tickets for ... **two tickets, please**
искам три билета за ... два билета, моля
eeskam tree bileta za ... *dva bileta, molya*

it's called ... **I've seen the trailer**
казва се ... виждал съм рекламата
kazva seh ... *veezhdal sum reklamata*

what time does it start? **what sort of music is it?**
в колко часа започва? какъв вид музика е това?
fkolko chasuh zapochva? *kakuf veed moozika eh tova?*

I'd like to go and see a show
искам да отида да видя някакво представление
eeskam da oteeda da veedya nyakakvo pretstavleni-eh

I'll find out whether there are still tickets available
ще видя дали още има билети
shteh veedya dalee oshteh eema bileti

do we need to book in advance?
трябва ли да запазим билети предварително?
tryabva lee da zapazim bileti predvareetelno?

how long is it on for?
колко време ще се дава?
kolko vremeh shteh seh dava?

are there tickets for another day?
има ли билети за друга дата?
eema lee bileti za drooga data?

I'd like to go to a bar with some live music
искам да отида на бар с музика на живо
eeskam da oteeda na bar smoozika na zheevo

are there any free concerts?
има ли някакви безплатни концерти?
eema lee nyakakvi besplatni kontserti?

Understanding

антракт	interval
билетен център	ticket office
каса	box office
независимо кино	arthouse cinema
народна музика	folk music
ограничен брой места	limited number of tickets
премиера	first night
резервации	bookings
хит	blockbuster

всички билети до ... са продадени
fseechki bileti do ... sa prodadeni
it's all booked up until ...

дават го в осем вечерта в Мултиплекс
davat go fosem vecherta fmooltipleks
it's on at 8pm at the Multiplex

за тази прожекция билетите са продадени
za tazi prozhektsi-ya biletiteh sa prodadeni
that showing's sold out

имаше много добри отзиви за това
eemasheh mnogo dobree otzivi za tova
it's had very good reviews

концерт на открито
kontsert na otkreeto
it's an open-air concert

моля, изключете мобилните телефони
molya, isklyucheteh mobeelniteh telefoni
please turn off your mobile phones

няма нужда да запазвате предварително
nyama noozhda da zapazvateh predvareetelno
there's no need to book in advance

пиесата трае час и половина заедно с антракта
pi-esata tra-eh chas ee poloveena za-edno santrakta
the play lasts an hour and a half, including the interval

пускат го следващата седмица
pooskat go sledvashtata sedmitsa
it comes out next week

PARTIES AND CLUBS

Expressing yourself

I'm having a little leaving party tonight
довечера организирам един малък купон за довиждане
dovechera organizeeram edeen maluk koopon za doveezhdaneh

should I bring something to drink?
да донеса ли нещо за пиене?
da donesuh lee neshto za pee-eneh?

we could go to a club afterwards
може да отидем в някой клуб след това
mozheh da oteedem fnyakoy kloop slet tova

GOING OUT

do you have to pay to get in?
плаща ли се вход?
plashta lee seh fHot?

I have to meet someone inside
имам среща с един човек вътре
eemam sreshta sedeen chovek vutreh

will you let me back in when I come back?
ще ме пуснете ли пак като се върна?
shteh meh poosneteh lee pak kato seh vurna?

can I buy you a drink?
да ви почерпя ли едно питие?
da vee pocherpya lee edno piti-eh?

do you come here often?
често ли идвате тук?
chesto lee eedvateh took?

no thanks, I don't smoke
не, благодаря, не пуша
neh, blagodaryuh, neh poosha

thanks, but I'm with my boyfriend
благодаря, но аз съм с приятеля си
blagodaryuh, no as sum spri-yatelya see

Understanding

пиенето безплатно
гардероб
пет лева куверт след
  полунощ

free drinks
cloakroom
BGN 5 entry after midnight

събираме се у Ани
subeerameh seh oo Ani
there's a party at Anne's place

може ли да те *(sg)*/ви *(pl)* изпратя?
mozheh lee da teh/vee ispratya?
can I see you home?

може ли да ви почерпя едно питие?
mozheh lee da vee pocherpya edno piti-eh?
can I buy you a drink?

имате ли запалка?
eemateh lee zapalka?
have you got a light?

имате ли една цигара?
eemateh lee edna tsigara?
have you got a cigarette?

TOURISM AND SIGHTSEEING

There is a tourist information office (**туристически информационен център** *tooristeecheski informatsi-onen tsentur*) in the centre of Sofia and in some other towns. There are free maps and English-language city guides in Sofia, available from all hotels and many restaurants. They are full of information about where to go and what to do. Similar guides are available on the Black Sea and in the towns of Plovdiv and Veliko Turnovo.

Museum opening hours vary, but are typically 10am to 6pm (closing for lunch in smaller towns and villages) six days a week. Monday is the usual day off. The exhibits are generally poorly labelled so it may be a good idea to opt for a guided tour. Most churches and monasteries welcome visitors, as long as you are appropriately dressed.

The basics

ancient древен *dreven*
antique антикварен *antikvaren*
area район *ra-yon*
cathedral катедрала *katedrala*
century век *vek*
church църква *tsurkva*
exhibition изложба *izlozhba*
fortress крепост *krepost*
gallery галерия *galeri-ya*
modern art модерно изкуство *moderno iskoostvo*
mosque джамия *dzhamee-ya*
museum музей *moozey*
painting картина *karteena*
park парк *park*
ruins (древни) останки *(drevni) ostanki*
sculpture скулптура *skoolptoora*
statue статуя *statoo-ya*

street map карта на града *karta na graduh*
synagogue синагога *sinagoga*
tour guide екскурзовод *ekskoorzovot*
tourist турист *(m)*, туристка *(f) tooreest/tooreestka*
tourist information centre туристическа информация
  tooristeecheska informatsi-ya
town centre център на града *tsentur na graduh*

Expressing yourself

I'd like some information on …
можете ли да ми дадете информация за …?
mozheteh lee da mee dadeteh informatsi-ya za …?

can you tell me where the tourist information centre is?
можете ли да ми кажете къде е туристическият информационен
център?
*mozheteh lee da mee kazheteh kudeh eh tooristeecheski-yat informatsi-onen
tsentur?*

do you have a street map of the town?
имате ли карта на града?
eemateh lee karta na graduh?

I was told there's an old fortress you can visit
казаха ми, че има една стара крепост, която може да се посети
kazaHa mee, cheh eema edna stara krepost, koyato mozheh da seh posetee

can you show me where it is on the map?
можете ли да ми я покажете на картата?
mozheteh lee da mee ya pokazheteh na kartata?

how do you get there?
как се стига до там?
kak seh steega do tam?

is it free?
без пари ли е?
bes paree lee eh?

Understanding

вие сте тук | you are here *(on a map)*
византийски | Byzantine
война | war
вход свободен | admission free

TOURISM, SIGHTSEEING

69

възраждане	Renaissance
затворено	closed
исторически	historical
нашествие	invasion
обиколка с екскурзовод	guided tour
отворено	open
параклис	chapel
римски	Roman
ремонт	renovation
реставрация	restoration work
средновековен	medieval
стария град	old town

следващата обиколка с екскурзовод започва в десет часа
sledvashtata obikolka sekskoorzovot zapochva vdeset chasuh
the next guided tour starts at 10 o'clock

трябва да питате като стигнете там
tryabva da peetateh kato steegneteh tam
you'll have to ask when you get there

MUSEUMS, EXHIBITIONS AND MONUMENTS

Expressing yourself

I've heard there's a very good ... exhibition on at the moment
чух, че има много хубава ... изложба в момента
chooH, cheh eema mnogo Hoobava ... izlozhba fmomenta

how much is it to get in?
колко се плаща за вход?
kolko seh plashta za fHot?

is this ticket valid for the exhibition as well?
билетът важи ли и за изложбата?
biletut vazhee lee eeh za izlozhbata?

are there any discounts for young people?
има ли намаление за младежи?
eema lee namaleni-eh za mladezhi?

is it open on Sundays?
отворено ли е в неделя?
otvoreno lee eh fnedelya?

I have a student card
имам студентска карта
eemam stoodentska karta

two concessions and one full price, please
два с намаление и един обикновен, моля
dva snamaleni-eh ee edeen obiknoven, molya

временна изложба	temporary exhibition
каса	ticket office
моля, пазете тишина	silence, please
моля, не пипайте	please do not touch
от тук	this way
постоянна изложба	permanent exhibition
слушалки	audioguide
снимането със светкавица забранено	no flash photography
снимането забранено	no photography

входът за музея е ...
fHodut za mooze-ya eh...
admission to the museum costs ...

носите ли студентската си карта?
nositeh lee stoodentskata see karta?
do you have your student card?

този билет важи и за изложбата
tozi bilet vazhee ee za izlozhbata
this ticket also allows you access to the exhibition

GIVING YOUR IMPRESSIONS

it was beautiful
беше красиво
besheh kraseevo

it was fantastic
беше фантастично
besheh fantasteechno

I really enjoyed it
много ми хареса
mnogo mee Haresa

I didn't like it that much
не ми хареса много
neh mee Haresa mnogo

it was a bit boring
беше малко скучно
besheh malko skoochno

it's expensive for what it is
скъпо е за това, което е
skupo eh za tova, koeto eh

I'm not really a fan of modern art
не съм голям любител на модерното изкуство
neh sum golyam lyubeetel na modernoto iskoostvo

it's very touristy
прекалено е комерсиално
prekaleno eh komersi-alno

it was really crowded
беше страшна навалица
besheh strashna navalitsa

we didn't have time to see everything
нямахме време да видим всичко
nyamaHmeh vremeh da veedim fseechko

Understanding

живописен	picturesque
известен	famous
типичен	typical
традиционен	traditional

брегът е абсолютно съсипан
bregut eh apsolyutno suseepan
the coast has been completely ruined

има чудесен изглед към целия град
eema choodesen eezglet kum tseli-ya grat
there's a wonderful view over the whole city

препоръчвам ви да отидете ...
preporuchvam vee da oteedeteh ...
I recommend going to …

станало е прекалено комерсиално
stanalo eh prekaleno komersi-alno
it's become a bit too touristy

трябва непременно да отидеш да видиш ...
tryabva nepremenno da oteedesh da veedish ...
you really must go and see …

SPORTS AND GAMES

The most popular spectator sport in Bulgaria is football. The two main teams are Levski Sofia, who play in blue, and CSKA, who are also based in Sofia and play in red with a star logo. Basketball is also widely played. Sports such as golf and tennis have become popular in recent years.

A third of Bulgaria is mountainous, making it an ideal destination for skiing in winter and hiking in summer. The capital city has its own ski resort on Vitosha mountain, clearly visible from the city centre. There are four main mountain ranges, all with a good network of mountain huts and hotels. In summer, the mountains are popular with walkers and climbers; Bulgaria can boast Mount Musala, the Balkan peninsula's highest peak. Potholing and fishing are other popular activities. Bulgaria's diverse flora and fauna make it a haven for nature lovers. There are plenty of websites (often with English content) with information on ecotourism, and increasing numbers of holidays catering for those who want to explore the country outside of the main resorts. The big coastal resorts are good for water sports, including diving and waterskiing. Card games such as bridge are popular, and chess is often played in city parks.

The basics

aerobics аеробика *a-erobika*
ball топка *topka*
backgammon табла *tabla*
badminton федербал *federbal*
basketball баскетбол *basketbol*
cards карти *karti*
chess шах *shaH*
cross-country skiing крос *kros*
cycling колоездене *kolo-ezdeneh*
downhill skiing ски спускане *skee spooskaneh*
football футбол *footbol*
hiking path маршрут *marshroot*
match мач *mach*

mountain biking планинско колоездене *planeensko kolo-ezdeneh*
pool *(game)* билярд *bilyart*
rugby ръгби *rugbi*
skating каране на кънки *karaneh na kunki*
skiing каране на ски *karaneh na skee*
snowboarding каране на сноуборд *karaneh na snowbort*
sport спорт *sport*
surfing сърфиране *surfeeraneh*
swimming плуване *ploovaneh*
swimming pool басейн *baseyn*
table football джаги *dzhagi*
table tennis тенис на маса *tenis na masa*
tennis тенис (на корт) *tenis (na kort)*
trip екскурзия *ekskoorzi-ya*
volleyball волейбол *voleybol*
to go hiking ходя на екскурзия/на планина *Hodya na ekskoorzi-ya/na planina*
to have a game of ... да изиграя една игра ... *da izigra-ya edna igra ...*
to play играя *igra-ya*, тренирам *treneeram*

Expressing yourself

I'd like to hire ... for an hour
искам да наема ... за един час
eeskam da na-ema ... za edeen chas

are there ... lessons available?
предлагат ли се уроци по ...?
predlagat lee seh oorotsi po ...?

how much is it per person per hour?
колко струва на час за един човек?
kolko stroova na chas za edeen chovek?

I've never done it before
никога не съм опитвал *(m)*/опитвала *(f)*
neekoga neh sum opeetval/opeetvala

I've done it once or twice, a long time ago
опитвал *(m)*/опитвала *(f)* съм един или два пъти, но много отдавна
opeetval/opeetvala sum edeen ilee dva puti, no mnogo otdavna

I'd like to go and watch a football match
искам да отида да гледам футболен мач
eeskam da oteeda da gledam footbolen mach

shall we stop for a picnic?
да си направим ли пикник тук?
da see napravim lee peeknik took?

we played ...
играхме ...
igraHmeh ...

I'm exhausted!
изморих се!
izmoreeH seh!

Understanding

... под наем   **... for hire**

застраховката е задължителна и струва ...
zastraHofkata eh zadulzheetelna ee stroova...
insurance is compulsory and costs ...

имате ли някакъв опит или сте съвсем начинаещ *(m)/*
начинаеща *(f)*?
eemateh lee nyakakuv opit ilee steh sufsem nachina-esht/nachina-eshta?
do you have any experience, or are you a complete beginner?

оставя се ... лева депозит
ostavya seh ... leva depozit
there is a deposit of ...

HIKING

Expressing yourself

are there any hiking paths around here?
има ли някакви планински маршрути тук?
eema lee nyakakvi planeenski marshrooti took?

can you recommend any good walks in the area?
можете ли да ни препоръчате приятни маршрути в околността?
mozheteh lee da nee preporuchateh pri-yatni marshrooti fokolnosta?

I've heard there's a nice walk by the lake
чувал (m)/чувала (f) съм, че има приятна пътека за разходка през
  гората
chooval/choovala sum, cheh eema pri-yatna puteka za rasHotka pres gorata

we're looking for a short walk somewhere round here
търсим немного дълъг маршрут за разходка наоколо
tursim nemnogo dulug marshroot za rasHotka na-okolo

can I hire hiking boots?
има ли туристически обувки под наем?
eema lee tooristeecheski oboofki pod na-em?

how long does the hike take?
колко дълго е изкачването?
kolko dulgo eh iskachvaneto?

is it very steep?
много ли е стръмно?
mnogo lee eh strumno?

where's the start of the path?
откъде започва пътеката?
otkudeh zapochva putekata?

is the path waymarked?
маркирана ли е пътеката?
markeerana lee eh putekata?

is it a circular path?
в кръг ли върви пътеката?
fkruk lee vurvee putekata?

Understanding

екскурзионно летуване   hiking holiday
средно дълъг маршрут   average duration (of walk)

носи (sg)/носете (pl) яке за дъжд и удобни обувки
nosee/noseteh yakeh za dusht ee oodobni oboofki
bring a waterproof jacket and some walking shoes

около три часа път с почивките
okolo tree chasa put spocheefkiteh
it's about a three-hour walk including rest stops

SPORTS AND GAMES

SKIING AND SNOWBOARDING

Expressing yourself

I'd like to hire skis, poles and boots
искам да взема ски, щеки и обувки под наем
eeskam da vzema skee, shteki ee oboofki pod na-em

I'd like to hire a snowboard
искам да взема сноуборд под наем
eeskam da vzema snowbort pod na-em

they're too big/small
твърде големи/малки са
tvurdeh golemi/malki sa

a day pass
дневна карта
dnevna karta

I'm a complete beginner
аз съм съвсем начинаещ *(m)*/начинаеща *(f)*
as sum sufsem nachina-esht/nachina-eshta

Understanding

кабинков лифт	cable car
карта за лифта	lift pass
котва	T-bar
седалков лифт	chair lift
ски влек	drag lift
ски лифт	ski lift
чинийка	button lift

OTHER SPORTS

Expressing yourself

where can we hire bikes?
откъде можем да вземем велосипеди под наем?
otkudeh mozhem da vzemem velosipedi pod na-em?

are there any cycle paths?
има ли алея за велосипедисти?
eema lee ale-ya za velosipedeesti?

does anyone have a football?
някой има ли футболна топка?
nyakoy eema lee footbolna topka?

which team do you support?
за кой отбор си *(sg)*/сте *(pl)*?
za koy otbor see/steh?

I support ...
аз съм за ...
as sum za …

is there an open-air swimming pool?
има ли басейн на открито?
eema lee baseyn na otkreeto?

I've never been diving before
никога не съм плувал *(m)*/плувала *(f)* под вода
neekoga neh sum plooval/ploovala pod voda

I'd like to take beginners' sailing lessons
искам да се запиша за уроци по платноходство за начинаещи
eeskam da seh zapeesha za oorotsi po platnoHotstvo za nachina-eshti

I run for half an hour every morning
тичам половин час всяка сутрин
teecham poloveen chas fsyaka sootrin

what do I do if the kayak capsizes?
какво да направя, ако кануто се обърне?
kakvo da napravya, ako kanooto seh oburneh?

Understanding

за първи път ли яздите кон?
za purvi put lee yazditeh kon?
is this the first time you've been horse-riding?

играете ли баскетбол?
igra-eteh lee basketbol?
do you play basketball?

има тенискорт близо до гарата
eema teniskort bleezo do garata
there's a public tennis court not far from the station

можете ли да плувате?
mozheteh lee da ploovateh?
can you swim?

тенискортът е зает
teniskortut eh za-et
the tennis court's occupied

INDOOR GAMES

Expressing yourself

shall we have a game of cards?
искате ли да играем карти?
eeskateh lee da igra-em karti?

does anyone know any good card games?
някой знае ли интересни игри на карти?
nyakoy zna-eh lee interesni igree na karti?

is anyone up for a game of Monopoly®?
иска ли някой да играе на Монополи?
eeska lee nyakoy da igra-eh na monopoli?

it's your turn
твой (sg)/ваш (pl) ред е
tvoy/vash ret eh

Understanding

имате ли карти?
eemateh lee karti?
do you have a pack of cards?

можете ли да играете шах?
mozheteh lee da igra-eteh shaH?
do you know how to play chess?

хайде да …
Haydeh da …
let's …

Some informal expressions

беше голям кеф *besheh golyam kef* it was fantastic
капнал съм *kapnal sum* I'm shattered
той ме разби *toy meh razbee* he thrashed me
хайде на бас *Hayde na bas* I bet you
хващам се на бас *Hvashtam seh na bas* to bet someone

SHOPPING

Food stores are generally open daily from 7am to 8pm, and sometimes 24 hours a day. Most other shops are open from 10am to 7pm Monday to Saturday, and sometimes on Sunday as well. In towns and cities there are markets all day, every day. You can haggle at open markets and souvenir stalls but not in shops. Take plenty of cash as few shops accept credit cards. Shoes are in European sizes. Bulgarian clothes sizes differ from the generally accepted European sizes (see Conversion Tables, pages 191-2).

In larger shops you should be able to bring goods back and exchange them for something of the same value as long as you keep your till receipt, but it is almost unheard of for a shop to return money, even for faulty goods.

Some informal expressions

без пари *bes paree* bargain
измама *izmama* con
менте *menteh* fake
пиратски *piratski* pirated
струва майка си и баща си *stroova mayka see ee bashta see*
it costs an arm and leg

The basics

bakery фурна *foorna*
baker's хлебарница *Hlebarnitsa*
butcher's месарница *mesarnitsa*
cash desk каса *kasa*
cheap евтин *eftin*
checkout каса *kasa*
clothes дрехи *dreHi*
department store универсален магазин *ooniversalen magazeen*
expensive скъп *skup*
gram грам *gram*
greengrocer's плод зеленчук *plot zelenchook*

hypermarket хипермаркет *Heepermarket*
kilo кило *kilo*
present подарък *podaruk*
price цена *tsena*
receipt бележка *beleshka*
refund връщане на парите *vrushtaneh na pareeteh*
sales assistant продавач *(m) prodavach*, продавачка *(f) prodavachka*
sales разпродажба *rasprodazhba*
shop магазин *magazeen*
shopping centre търговски център *turgofski tsentur*
souvenir сувенир *sooveneer*
supermarket супермаркет *soopermarket*
to buy купувам *koopoovam*
to cost струвам *stroovam*
to pay плащам *plashtam*
to sell продавам *prodavam*

Expressing yourself

is there a supermarket near here?
има ли супермаркет наблизо?
eema lee soopermarket nableezo?

where can I buy cigarettes?
откъде мога да купя цигари?
otkudeh moga da koopya tsigari?

I'd like ...
искам ...
eeskam ...

I'm looking for ...
търся ...
tursya ...

do you sell ...?
продавате ли ...?
prodavateh lee ...?

can you order it for me?
можете ли да ми го поръчате?
mozheteh lee da mee go poruchateh?

do you know where I might find some ...?
знаете ли къде мога да намеря ...?
zna-eteh lee kudeh moga da namerya...?

how much is this?
колко струва?
kolko stroova?

I'll take it
ще го взема
shteh go vzema

I haven't got enough money
нямам достатъчно пари
nyamam dostatuchno paree

I haven't got much money
нямам много пари
nyamam mnogo paree

that's everything, thanks
това е всичко, благодаря
tova eh fseechko, blagodaryuh

can I have a (plastic) bag?
можете ли да ми дадете (найлонова) торбичка?
mozheteh lee da mee dadeteh (naylonova) torbeechka?

I think you've made a mistake with my change
мисля, че не ми връщате точно
meeslya, cheh neh mee vrushtateh tochno

Understanding

затворено в неделя
обедна почивка от **13** до **14**
отворено от ... до ...
промоция/акция
разпродажба

closed Sundays
lunch break from 1pm to 2pm
open from ... to ...
special offer
sales

искате ли торбичка/пликче?
eeskateh lee torbeechka/pleekcheh?
would you like a bag?

нещо друго?
neshto droogo?
will there be anything else?

PAYING

Expressing yourself

where do I pay?
къде да платя?
kudeh da platyuh?

how much do I owe you?
колко ви дължа?
kolko vee dulzhuh?

could you write it down for me, please?
бихте ли го написали, моля?
beeHteh lee go napeesali, molya?

can I pay by credit card?
може ли да платя с кредитна карта?
mozheh lee da platyuh skreditna karta?

I'll pay in cash
ще платя в брой
shteh platyuh vbroy

I'm sorry, I haven't got any change
съжалявам, нямам дребни
suzhalyavam, nyamam drebni

can I have a receipt?
може ли да ми дадете бележка?
mozheh lee da mee dadeteh beleshka?

Understanding

платете на касата | pay at the cash desk

имате ли документ за самоличност?
eemateh lee dokooment za samoleechnost?
have you got any ID?

имате ли стотинки?
eemateh lee stoteenki?
do you have any coins?

как ще платите?
kak shteh plateeteh?
how would you like to pay?

моля, подпишете тук
molya, potpisheteh took
could you sign here, please?

само точни пари
samo tochni paree
exact change only

FOOD

Expressing yourself

where can I buy food around here?
откъде мога да купя нещо за ядене наблизо?
otkudeh moga da koopya neshto za yadeneh nableezo?

is there a market?
има ли пазар?
eema lee pazar?

is there a bakery around here?
има ли хлебарница наблизо?
eema lee Hlebarnitsa nableezo?

I'm looking for the biscuit aisle
търся стелажите с бисквити
tursya stelazhiteh zbiskveeti

I'd like some of that sheep's cheese
искам малко от това овче сирене
eeskam malko ot tova ofcheh seereneh

it's for four people
за четири души е
za chetiri dooshi eh

a kilo of apples, please
кило ябълки, моля
kilo yabulki, molya

can I taste it?
може ли да опитам?
mozheh lee da opeetam?

I'd like 200 grams of ham
искам 200 грама шунка
eeskam dvesta grama shoonka

about 300 grams
около 300 грама
okolo treesta grama

a bit less/more
малко по-малко/повече, моля
malko po-malko/poveche, molya

does it travel well?
трайно ли е?
trayno lee eh?

Understanding

екологично чиста храна	organic food
национални специалитети	local specialities
(магазин за) деликатеси	delicatessen
домашен	homemade
годно до …	best before …

има един плод зеленчук на ъгъла, който работи до късно
eema edeen plot zelenchook na ugula, koyto raboti do kusno
there's a grocer's just on the corner that's open late

има пазар всеки ден до 13 часа
eema pazar fseki den do trinayset chasuh
there's a market every day until 1pm

CLOTHES

Expressing yourself

I'm looking for the menswear section
търся мъжки дрехи
tursya mushki dreHi

no thanks, I'm just looking
не, благодаря, само гледам
neh, blagodaryuh, samo gledam

can I try it on?
може ли да го пробвам?
mozheh lee da go probvam?

I'd like to try the one in the window
искам да пробвам това на витрината
eeskam da probvam tova na vitreenata

I take a size 39 (in shoes)
нося трийсет и девети номер
nosya treeyset ee deveti nomer

where are the changing rooms?
къде е пробната?
kudeh eh probnata?

it doesn't fit
не ми става
neh mee stava

it's too big/small
много ми е голямо/малко
mnogo mee eh golyamo/malko

do you have it in another colour?
имате ли друг цвят?
eemateh lee drook tsvyat?

do you have it in a smaller/bigger size?
имате ли по-голям/по-малък размер?
eemateh lee po-golyam/po-maluk razmer?

do you have them in red?
имате ли ги в червено?
eemateh lee gee fcherveno?

yes, that's fine, I'll take them
да, става, ще ги взема
da, stava, shteh gee vzema

no, I don't like it
не, не ми харесва
neh, neh mee Haresva

I'll think about it
ще помисля
shteh pomeeslya

I'd like to return this, it doesn't fit
искам да върна това, не ми става
eeskam da vurna tova, neh mee stava

this ... has a hole in it, can I get a refund?
този/тази/това ... има дупка, може ли да ми върнете парите?
tozi/tazi/tova ... eema doopka, mozheh lee da mee vurneteh pareeteh?

Understanding

бельо	lingerie
дамски дрехи	ladieswear
детски дрехи	children's clothes
мъжки дрехи	menswear
намаление	discount
отворено в неделя	open Sunday
пробна	changing rooms
стоки с намаление не се връщат	sale/reduced items cannot be returned

здравейте, мога ли да ви помогна?
zdraveyteh, moga lee da vee pomogna?
hello, can I help you?

имаме го само в синьо и черно
eemameh go samo fseenyo ee cherno
we only have it in blue or black

може да го върнете, ако не ви става
mozheh da go vurneteh, ako neh vee stava
you can bring it back if it doesn't fit

отива ви
oteeva vee
it suits you

този размер свърши
tozi razmer svurshi
we don't have any left in that size

това е точно вашият размер
tova eh tochno vashi-yut razmer
it's a good fit

SOUVENIRS AND PRESENTS

Expressing yourself

I'm looking for a present to take home
търся нещо за спомен
tursya neshto za spomen

I'd like something that's easy to transport
търся нещо, което да може да се пренася лесно
tursya neshto ko-eto mozheh da seh prenasya lesno

it's for a little girl of four
за едно момиченце на четири години
za edno momeechentseh na chetiri godeeni

could you gift-wrap it for me?
бихте ли го опаковали като подарък?
beeHteh lee go opakovali kato podaruk?

Understanding

битов предмет	traditionally made product
дървен/сребърен/златен/вълнен	made of wood/silver/gold/wool
ръчен	handmade

за подарък ли е?
za podaruk lee eh?
is it for a present?

колко сте готов/готова да похарчите?
kolko steh gotov/gotova da poHarchiteh?
how much do you want to spend?

това е типично за този район
tova eh tipeechno za tozi ra-yon
it's typical of the region

PHOTOS

ℹ️

Prices for films and developing are lower than in the UK. Shops offering the same technology and brands as those in western Europe are easy to find in cities. More and more photo developers will now burn digital photos to CD from a memory card.

The basics

black and white чернобяла снимка *chernobyala sneemka*
camera фотоапарат *foto-aparat*
colour цветна снимка *tsvetna sneemka*
CD сиди *seedee*, компактдиск *kompaktdisk*
copy копие *kopi-eh*
digital camera цифров фотоапарат *tseefrof foto-aparat*
disposable (camera) за еднократна употреба *za ednokratna oopotreba*
exposure бленда *blenda*
film филм *feelm*
flash светкавица *svetkavitsa*
glossy гланцов *glantsof*
matte матов *matof*
memory card памет карта *pamet karta*
negative негатив *negateef*
passport photo снимка за паспорт *sneemka za pasport*
reprint копие *kopi-eh*
slide диапозитив *di-apoziteef*
to copy копирам *kopeeram*
to get photos developed проявявам снимки *pro-yavyavam sneemki*
to take a photo/photos снимам *sneemam*

Expressing yourself

could you take a photo of us, please?
може ли да ни снимате, моля?
mozheh lee da nee sneemateh, molya?

you just have to press this button
трябва само да натиснете това копче
tryabva samo da nateesneteh tova kopcheh

I'd like a 200 ASA colour film
един цветен филм двеста АСА, ако обичате
edeen tsveten feelm dvesta asa, ako obeechateh

do you have black and white films?
имате ли чернобели филми?
eemateh lee chernobeli feelmi?

how much is it to develop a film of 36 photos?
колко струва проявяването на филм с трийсет и шест пози?
kolko stroova pro-yavyavaneto na feelm streeyset ee shest pozi?

I'd like to have this film developed
бих искал *(m)*/искала *(f)* да проявите този филм
beeh eeskal/eeskala da proyaveeteh tozi feelm

I'd like extra copies of some of the photos
искам допълнителни копия на някои от снимките
eeskam dopulneetelni kopi-ya na nyako-i ot sneemkiteh

three copies of this one and two of this one
три копия от тази и две от тази
tree kopi-ya ot tazi ee dveh ot tazi

do you print digital photos here?
можете ли да правите цифрови снимки тук?
mozheteh lee da praviteh tseefrovi sneemki took?

can you put these photos on a CD for me?
можете ли да ми прехвърлите тези снимки върху сиди?
mozheteh lee da mee preHvurliteh tezi sneemki vurHoo seedee?

I've come to pick up my photos
идвам да получа снимките си
eedvam da poloocha sneemkiteh see

I've got a problem with my camera
фотоапаратът ми не е наред
foto-aparatut mee neh eh naret

I don't know what it is
не знам какъв е проблемът
neh znam kakuf eh problemut

the flash doesn't work
светкавицата не работи
svetkavitsata neh raboti

Understanding

експресни услуги   express service
проявяване за един час   photos developed in one hour
стандартен размер   standard format
снимки на сиди   photos on CD

може би батерията е свършила
mozheh bee bateri-yata eh svurshila
maybe the battery's dead

имаме машина за копиране на цифрови снимки
eemameh masheena za kopeeraneh na tseefrovi sneemki
we have a machine for printing digital photos

името ви, моля?
eemeto vee, molya?
what's the name, please?

за кога ги искате?
za koga gee eeskateh?
when do you want them for?

можем да ги направим за един час
mozhem da gee napravim za edeen chas
we can print them in an hour

снимките ви ще са готови в четвъртък по обяд
sneemkiteh vee shteh sa gotovi fchetvurtuk po obyat
your photos will be ready on Thursday at noon

BANKS

The national currency is the **лев** *lef* (plural **лева** *leva*). The word for money is **пари** *paree* (a plural word). Be sure to place the stress on the last syllable, as *pari* means something quite different (it's hot). There are 100 **стотинки** *stoteenki* coins to one lev. You can change money in banks (open Monday to Friday from 9am to 5pm) or in bureaux de change, but be aware that bureaux de change have become infamous for various scams over the last few years so use them only if there is no bank available. Commission fees are not charged but exchange rates vary from one place to another.

Cash machines are plentiful in all but the most out of the way locations and money can be withdrawn in the national currency with a credit card. Many shops and restaurants in cities and resorts already take credit cards. Cheques are not used in Bulgaria. Note that the British pound may be referred to in Bulgaria as **британска лира** *britanska leera* (plural **британски лири** *britanski leeri*).

Some informal expressions

два/три бона *dva/tree bona* two/three thousand
два/три кинта *dva/tree keenta* two/three levs
в зелено *vzeleno* in dollars
кинти *keenti* dough, cash
колко кинта? *kolko keenta?* how much money?

The basics

bank банка *banka*
bank account банкова сметка *bankova smetka*
banknote банкнота *banknota*
bureau de change обменно бюро *obmenno byuro*
cashpoint банкомат *bankomat*
change *(money given back)* ресто *resto*; *(small change)* дребни *drebni*

cheque чек *chek*
coin монета *moneta*
commission комисионна *komisi-onna*
credit card кредитна карта *kreditna karta*
PIN (number) пин код *pin kot*
transfer прехвърляне *preHvurlyaneh*
Travellers Cheques® травълър чек *travulur chek*
withdrawal теглене *tegleneh*
to change обменям *obmenyam*
to transfer прехвърлям *preHvurlyam*
to withdraw тегля *teglya*

Expressing yourself

where can I get some money changed?
къде мога да обменя пари?
kudeh moga da obmenyuh paree?

are banks open on Saturdays?
отворени ли са банките в събота?
otvoreni lee sa bankiteh fsubota?

I'm looking for a cashpoint
търся банкомат
tursya bankomat

I'd like to change £100
искам да обменя сто лири
eeskam da obmenyuh sto leeri

what commission do you charge?
каква е комисионната?
kakva eh komisi-onnata?

I'd like to transfer some money
искам да прехвърля пари
eeskam da preHvurlya paree

I'd like to report the loss of my credit card
искам да съобщя, че съм изгубил кредитната си карта
eeskam da su-opshtyuh, cheh sum izgoobil kreditnata see karta

the cashpoint has swallowed my card
банкоматът глътна картата ми
bankomatut glutna kartata mee

Understanding

моля, поставете вашата карта
please insert your card

моля, въведете вашия пин код
please enter your PIN number

моля, натиснете бутона срещу желаната сума
please select amount for withdrawal

желаете ли разписка?
would you like a receipt?

теглене без разписка
withdrawal without receipt

не работи
out of service

теглене с разписка
withdrawal with receipt

моля, изберете желаната сума
please select the amount you require

други услуги
other services

POST OFFICES

Letter boxes are found inside or outside post offices (**поща** *poshta*). They may be marked with the destination: **за чужбина** *za choozhbeena* (abroad), **за страната** *za stranata* (domestic) and sometimes the name of the city (**София** Sofia, **Пловдив** Plovdiv, **Варна** Varna etc). Post offices are generally open Monday to Saturday from 9am to 7pm, or sometimes until 8pm in summer. In big cities they are also open on Sundays until midday. Envelopes and stamps are mainly sold in post offices, and you will have to specify whether the destination is **България** (Bulgaria) or **Европа** (Europe). For other continents, and for registered mail (**препоръчана поща** *preporuchana poshta*) and parcels, you will need to speak to a counter assistant. There are three classes of post at different prices: **обикновена поща** *obiknovena poshta* (normal), **бърза поща** *burza poshta* (fast) and **експресна поща** *ekspresna poshta* (express).

The basics

airmail въздушна поща *vuzdooshna poshta*
envelope плик *pleek*
letter писмо *pismo*
mail поща *poshta*
parcel колет *kolet*
post поща *poshta*
postbox пощенска кутия *poshtenska kootee-ya*
postcard картичка *kartichka*
postcode пощенски код *poshtenski kot*
post office поща *poshta*
registered letter препоръчано писмо *preporuchano pismo*
stamp марка *marka*
to post пускам *pooskam*
to send пращам/да изпратя *prashtam/da izpratya*
to write пиша/да напиша *peesha/da napeesha*

Expressing yourself

is there a post office around here?
има ли поща наблизо?
eema lee poshta nableezo?

is there a postbox near here?
има ли пощенска кутия наблизо?
eema lee poshtenska kootee-ya nableezo?

is the post office open on Saturdays?
пощата работи ли в неделя?
poshtata raboti lee fnedelya?

what time does the post office close?
кога затварят пощата?
koga zatvaryat poshtata?

do you sell stamps?
продавате ли марки?
prodavateh lee marki?

I'd like ... stamps for the UK, please
може ли ... марки за Великобритания, моля
mozheh lee… marki za velikobritani-ya, molya

how long will it take to arrive?
за колко време ще пристигне?
za kolko vremeh shteh pristeegneh?

where can I buy envelopes?
къде мога да купя пликове?
kudeh moga da koopya pleekoveh?

is there any post for me?
има ли поща за мене?
eema lee poshta za meneh?

Understanding

Making sense of addresses

When addressing mail to be sent within Bulgaria, you can use either the Cyrillic or the Roman alphabet as the locals can read both.

A typical Bulgarian address looks like this:

Иван Атанасов
ул. "Марица" 10, вх. "А", ет. 3, ап. 16
4003 Пловдив
България

Note that the street name is given in inverted commas and the house number comes after it, not before. The recipient's address should be written in the bottom right-hand corner. The sender's address should be written in the top left-hand corner.

Some common abbreviations:
ап. = апартамент apartment
бл. = блок block
бул. = булевард boulevard
вх. = вход entrance (to a building)
гр. = град town, city
ет. = етаж floor
ж. к. = жилищен комплекс housing complex, residential area
кв. = квартал quarter, neighbourhood
пл. = площад square
ул. = улица street

внимание чупливо	handle with care
податель	sender
последно събиране	last collection
първо събиране	first collection
чупливо	fragile

ще пристигне за три до пет дни
shteh pristeegneh za tree do pet dnee
it'll take between three and five days

INTERNET CAFÉS AND E-MAIL

www

Most Bulgarians now have an e-mail address. However, fewer people have computers at home, so even small villages usually have at least one Internet café (known as *ee*nternet *kloop* or *ee*nternet *kafeh*). These usually work well, though connections can sometimes be slow in remote areas. Many Internet cafés stay open until 9pm or later, while in big cities many are open 24 hours. Bulgarian Telecommunications Company (**БТК**) centres tend to have the most reliable connections. Hotels do not usually offer Internet access unless they are very upmarket, though Wi-Fi is already available in some locations in Sofia. Most computers have a QWERTY keyboard, but with both Roman and Cyrillic alphabets. You can toggle between the two by pressing Ctrl or Shift+Alt.

The basics

at sign маймунка *maymoonka*, кльомба *klyomba*
e-mail address имейл адрес *ee*meyl *adres*
Internet café интернет кафе *ee*nternet *kafeh*
key клавиш *klaveesh*
keyboard клавиатура *klavi-atoora*
to copy копирам *kopeeram*
to cut изразвам *izryazvam*
to delete изтривам/да изтрия *istreevam/da istree-ya*
to download тегля *teglya*
to e-mail пращам имейл *prashtam eemeyl*
to paste поставям *postavyam*
to receive получавам *poloochavam*
to save запазвам *zapazvam*
to send an e-mail пращам/да изпратя имейл *prashtam/da ispratya eemeyl*

Expressing yourself

is there an Internet café near here?
има ли интернет клуб наблизо?
eema lee eenternet kloop nableezo?

do you have an e-mail address?
имаш (sg)/имате (pl) ли имейл адрес?
eemash/eemateh lee eemeyl adres?

how do I get online?
как да се включа в мрежата?
kak da seh fklyucha fmrezhata?

I'd just like to check my e-mails
искам само да проверя пощата си
eeskam samo da proveryuh poshtata see

would you mind helping me, I'm not sure what to do
бихте ли ми помогнали, не знам какво да направя
beeHteh lee mee pomognali, ne znam kakvo da napravya

I can't find the at sign on this keyboard
не мога да намеря маймунката на тази клавиатура
ne moga da namerya maymoonkata na tazi klavi-atoora

it's not working
не работи
neh raboti

there's something wrong with the computer, it's frozen
на този компютър му има нещо, блокира
na tozi kompyutur moo eema neshto, blokeera

how much will it be for half an hour?
колко струва за половин час?
kolko stroova za poloveen chas?

when do I pay?
кога се плаща?
koga seh plashta?

Understanding

входяща поща	inbox
електронна поща	e-mail
изходяща поща	outbox

попитайте, ако нещо не ви е ясно
*pop**ee**tayteh, ak**o** n**e**shto neh vee eh **ya**sno*
just ask if you're not sure what to do

просто вкарайте паролата, за да влезете
*pr**o**sto fk**a**rayteh par**o**lata, za da vl**e**zeteh*
just enter this password to log on

ще трябва да изчакате 20 минути
*shteh tr**ya**bva da isch**a**kateh dv**ay**set min**oo**ti*
you'll have to wait for 20 minutes or so

TELEPHONE

(i)

To call the UK from Bulgaria, dial 00 44 followed by the area code (minus the first zero) and phone number. The international dialling code for Ireland is 00 353, and for the US and Canada it is 001. To call Bulgaria from abroad, dial 00 359 followed by the number given to you by your Bulgarian contact – they usually include the area code. Within Bulgaria, a list of area codes can be found at the local post office. No area code is needed for local calls. Phone numbers are read out in pairs (sometimes in threes) of digits, for example 44-62-08 *cheteeriset ee chetiri, sheyset ee dveh, noola osem*. The number for directory enquiries (**справки** *sprafki*) is **144**.

You can make calls from street phone boxes or from telephone centres (**телефонни кабини** *telefonni kabeenki*), which are recommended for international calls. You can buy phone cards (worth 25, 50 or 100 units) at newspaper kiosks and post offices to be used in the blue and orange phone boxes on the streets. For international calls, they take Visa® and Mastercard® (instructions are given in English). Cards that give you a code to type in are also widely available. Coin-operated phone boxes (**монетен телефон** *moneten telefon*) or those which take tokens (**телефон с жетони** *telefon z-zhetoni*) are becoming less and less common and are mainly found in post offices, which sell the required tokens.

If you have a mobile phone, you may find it more convenient to buy a prepaid card from one of the local mobile phone operators (Globul, Mtel and Vivatel). You can buy these in any mobile phone shop or newsagent.

Note that goodbye on the phone is **дочуване** *dochoovaneh* (literally "till we hear one another again") and not **довиждане** *doveezhdaneh* ("till we see one another again") as it is when you are face to face with someone.

The basics

answering machine телефонен секретар *telefonen sekretar*
call обаждане *obazhdaneh*; разговор *razgovor*
directory enquiries телефонни услуги *telefonni oosloogi*
hello ало *alo*

international call международен разговор *mezhdoonaroden razgovor*
local call градски разговор *gratski razgovor*
message съобщение *su-opshteni-eh*
mobile мобиелн телефон *mobeelen telefon*
national call междуградски разговор *mezhdoogratski razgovor*
phone book телефонен указател *telefonen ookazatel*
phone box телефонна кабина *telefonna kabeena*
phone call обаждане по телефона *obazhdaneh po telefona*
phone number телефонен номер *telefonen nomer*
phonecard фонокарта *fonokarta*
ringtone сигнал *signal*
telephone телефон *telefon*
text message есемес *esemes (SMS)*
top-up card предплатена карта *pretplatena karta*
Yellow Pages® Жълти страници *zhulti stranitsi*
to call somebody обаждам се/да се обадя на някого *obazhdam seh/da seh obadya na nyakogo*

Expressing yourself

where can I buy a phonecard?
откъде мога да купя фонокарта, моля?
otkudeh moga da koopya fonokarta, molya?

a 15-leva top-up card, please
една предплатена карта за петнайсет лева, ако обичате
edna pretplatena karta za petnayset leva, ako obeechateh

I'd like to make a reverse-charge call
искам да се обадя за тяхна сметка
eeskam da seh obadya za tyaHna smetka

is there a payphone near here, please?
има ли наблизо телефонен автомат, моля?
eema lee nableezo telefonen aftomat, molya?

can I plug my phone in here to recharge it?
може ли да включа телефона си тук, за да го заредя?
mozheh lee da fklyucha telefona see took, za da go zaredyuh?

do you have a mobile number?
имате ли мобилен телефон?
eemateh lee mobeelen telefon?

where can I contact you?
къде мога да ви се обадя?
kudeh moga da vee seh obadya?

did you get my message?
получихте ли съобщението ми?
poloochiHteh lee su-opshteni-eto mee?

Understanding

ваучер
грешка

top-up card
wrong number

изпрати ми есемес
ispratee mee esemes
send me a text message

моля, натиснете бутон диез
molya, natisneteh booton di-es
please press the hash key

набрали сте несъществуващ телефонен номер
nabrali steh nesushtestvoovasht telefonen nomer
the number you have dialled has not been recognized

телефонът е изключен по технически причини
telefonut eh isklyuchen po teHneecheski pricheeni
the telephone is switched off for technical reasons

MAKING A CALL

Expressing yourself

hello, this is David Brown (speaking)
ало, обажда се David Brown
alo, obazhda seh deyvid bra-oon

hello, could I speak to ..., please?
ало, може ли да говоря с ...?
alo, mozheh lee da govorya s ...?

hello, is that Maria?
ало, Мария ли е?
alo, maree-ya lee eh?

do you speak English?
говорите ли английски?
govoriteh lee angleeyski?

could you speak more slowly, please?
може ли да говорите по-бавно, моля?
mozheh lee da govoriteh po-bavno, molya?

I can't hear you, could you speak up, please?
не ви чувам, моля, говорете по-високо
neh vee choovam, molya, govoreteh po-visoko

could you tell him/her I called?
моля, кажете му/й, че съм се обаждал
molya, kazheteh moo/ee, cheh sum seh obazhdal

could you ask him/her to call me back?
моля, кажете му/й да ми се обади
molya, kazheteh moo/ee da mee seh obadi

my name is … and my number is …
казвам се ..., а телефонът ми е ...
kazvam seh …, a telefonut mee eh …

do you know when he/she might be available?
знаете ли, кога мога да се свържа с него/нея?
zna-eteh lee, koga moga da seh svurzha snego/sne-ya

I'll call back later
ще се обадя пак по-късно
shteh seh obadya pak po-kusno

thank you, goodbye
благодаря, дочуване
blagodaryuh, dochoovaneh

Understanding

имате грешка
eemateh greshka
you've got the wrong number

искате ли да оставите съобщение?
eeskateh lee da ostaviteh su-opshteni-eh?
do you want to leave a message?

кой се обажда?
koy seh obazhda?
who's calling?

почакайте
pochakayteh
hold on

сега ще ви се обади
sega shteh vee seh obadi
I'll just hand you over to him/her

той/тя не е вкъщи в момента
toy/tya neh eh fkushti fmomenta
he's/she's not here at the moment

ще му/ѝ кажа, че сте се обаждали
shteh moo/ee kazha, cheh steh seh obazhdali
I'll tell him/her you called

ще му/ѝ кажа да ви се обади
shteh moo/ee kazha da vee seh obadi
I'll ask him/her to call you back

PROBLEMS

Expressing yourself

I don't know the code
не знам кода
neh znam koda

it's engaged
заето е
za-eto eh

there's no reply
не отговаря
neh otgovarya

I couldn't get through
не можах да се свържа
neh mozhaH da seh svurzha

I don't have much credit left on my phone
нямам много пари в сметката
nyamam mnogo paree fsmetkata

we're about to get cut off
скоро ще ни прекъснат
skoro shteh nee prekusnat

the reception's really bad
връзката е много лоша
vruskata eh mnogo losha

I can't get a signal
няма сигнал
nyama signal

Understanding

едва ви чувам
edva vee choovam
I can hardly hear you

линията е лоша
leeni-yata eh losha
it's a bad line

> **Common abbreviations**
> **вътр.** = вътрешен extension   **моб.** = мобилен mobile (number)
> **дом.** = домашен home (number)   **служ.** = служебен work (number)

TELEPHONE

HEALTH

Pharmacies are open from 8am to 7pm, though some in big cities are open 24 hours a day (**денонощна аптека** *denonoshtna apteka*), thus eliminating the need for duty pharmacies (**дежурна аптека** *dezhoorna apteka*). In Bulgaria, you have to see a GP before you can see a specialist. However, there are many private clinics in the cities and you can see any specialist there without waiting. Facilities in public hospitals can be rather dilapidated, but this is less of a problem in the private sector. Doctors in hospitals often speak English. In case of emergency, dial **150.**

The basics

allergy алергия *alergi-ya*
ambulance линейка *lineyka*, бърза помощ *burza pomosht*
aspirin аспирин *aspireen*
blood кръв *kruf*
broken счупен *schoopen*
burn изгаряне *izgaryaneh*
casualty (department) спешна помощ *speshna pomosht*
chemist's аптека *apteka*
condom презерватив *prezervateef*
dentist зъболекар *zubolekar*
diarrhoea диария *di-ari-ya*
doctor лекар *lekar*
emergency спешен случаи *speshen sloochay*
food poisoning хранително отравяне *Hraneetelno otravyaneh*
GP семеен лекар *seme-en lekar*, джипи *dzhipee*
gynaecologist гинеколог *ginekolok*
hospital болница *bolnitsa*
infection инфекция *infektsi-ya*
medicine лекарство *lekarstvo*
painkiller обезболяващо (лекарство) *obezbolyavashto (lekarstvo)*
periods менструация *menstroo-atsi-ya*
plaster лепенка *lepenka*, лейкопласт *leykoplast*
rash обрив *obrif*

spot пъпка *pupka*
sunburn слънчево изгаряне *slunchevo izgaryaneh*
surgical spirit медицински спирт *meditseenski speert*
tablet таблетка *tabletka*
temperature температура *temperatoora*
vaccination имунизация *imoonizatsi-ya*
wound рана *rana*
x-ray рентген *rentgen*
to disinfect дезинфекцирам *dezinfektseeram*
to faint припадам/да припадна *pripadam/da pripadna*
to vomit повръщам/да повърна *povrushtam/da povurna*

Expressing yourself

does anyone have an aspirin/a tampon/a plaster, by any chance?
има ли някой случайно аспирин/тампон/лепенка?
eema lee nyakoy sloochayno aspireen/tampon/lepenka?

I need to see a doctor
трябва да отида на лекар
tryabva da oteeda na lekar

where can I find a doctor?
къде има лекар?
kudeh eema lekar?

I'd like to make an appointment for today
искам да запазя час за днес
eeskam da zapazya chas za dnes

as soon as possible
колкото може по-бързо
kolkoto mozheh po-burzo

no, it doesn't matter
не, няма значение
neh, nyama znacheni-eh

can you send an ambulance to ...
можете ли да изпратите линейка на ...?
mozheteh lee da izpratiteh lineyka na ...?

I've broken my glasses
счупих си очилата
schoopiH see ochilata

I've lost a contact lens
изгубих си едната леща
izgoobiH see ednata leshta

Understanding

лекарски кабинет   doctor's surgery
рецепта   prescription

спешно отделение   casualty department

няма свободни часове преди четвъртък
nyama svobodni chasoveh predee chetvurtuk
there are no available appointments until Thursday

петък в три следобед удобно ли ви е?
petuk ftree sledobet oodobno lee vee eh?
is Friday at 3pm OK?

AT THE DOCTOR'S OR THE HOSPITAL

Expressing yourself

I have an appointment with Dr …
имам час за доктор ....
eemam chas za doktor …

I don't feel very well
не се чувствам много добре
neh seh choostvam mnogo dobreh

I feel very weak
отпаднал *(m)*/отпаднала *(f)* съм
otpadnal/otpadnala sum

I'm feeling dizzy
вие ми се свят
vee-eh mee seh sfyat

I don't know what it is
не знам какво ми е
neh znam kakvo mee eh

I've been bitten/stung by …
ухапа/ужили ме ...
ooHapa/oozheeli meh…

I've got a headache
боли ме главата
bolee meh glavata

I've got toothache/stomachache
боли ме зъбът/стомахът
bolee meh zubut/stomaHut

I've got a sore throat
боли ме гърлото
bolee meh gurloto

my back hurts
боли ме гърбът
bolee meh gurbut

it hurts
боли
bolee

it hurts here
боли тук
bolee took

I feel sick
гади ми се
gadi mee seh

it's got worse
става по-лошо
stava po-losho

it's been three days
от три дни
ot tree dnee

it started last night
от снощи
ot snoshti

it's never happened to me before
преди никога не ми се е случвало
predee neekoga neh mee seh eh sloochvalo

I've got a temperature
имам температура
eemam temperatoora

I have asthma
имам астма
eemam astma

I have a heart condition
имам сърдечно заболяване
eemam surdechno zabolyavaneh

I've been on antibiotics for a week and I'm not getting any better
пия антибиотик от една седмица, но нямам подобрение
pee-ya antibi-otik ot edna sedmitsa, no nyamam podobreni-eh

it itches
сърби
surbee

I'm on the pill
взимам противозачатъчни
vzeemam proteevozachatuchni

I'm ... months pregnant
бременна съм в ... месец
bremenna sum v ... mesets

I'm allergic to penicillin
алергичен (m)/алергична (f) съм към пеницилин
alergeechen/alergeechna sum kum penitsileen

I've twisted my ankle
изкълчих си глезена
iskulchiH see glezena

I fell and hurt my back
паднах и си ударих гърба
padnaH ee see oodariH gurba

I've had a blackout
загубих съзнание
zagoobiH suznani-eh

I've lost a filling
падна ми една пломба
padna mee edna plomba

is it serious?
сериозно ли е?
seri-ozno lee eh?

is it contagious?
заразно ли е?
zarazno lee eh?

how is he/she?
как е той/тя?
kak eh toy/tya?

how much do I owe you?
колко ви дължа?
kolko vee dulzuh?

can I have a receipt so I can get the money refunded?
може ли да получа фактура, за да си възстановя парите?
mozheh lee da poloocha faktoora, za da see vustanovyuh pareeteh?

Understanding

алергичен (m)/**алергична** (f) **ли сте към ...?**
alergeechen/alergeechna lee steh kum …?
are you allergic to …?

боли ли като натискам?
bolee lee kato nateeskam?
does it hurt when I press here?

дишайте дълбоко
deeshayteh dulboko
take a deep breath

взимате ли някакви други лекарства?
vzeematah lee nyakakvi droogi lekarstva?
are you taking any other medication?

елате пак при мен след една седмица
elateh pak pree men slet edna sedmitsa
come back and see me in a week

имате ли имунизация срещу ...?
eemateh lee imoonizatsi-ya sreshtoo …?
have you been vaccinated against …?

имате нужда от операция
eemateh noozhda ot operatsi-ya
you're going to need an operation

как се чувствате?
kak se choostvateh?
how are you feeling?

къде боли?
kudeh bolee?
where does it hurt?

легнете, моля
legneteh, molya
lie down, please

моля, заповядайте в чакалнята
molya, zapovyadayteh fchakalnyata
if you'd like to take a seat in the waiting room

сигурно ще се оправите след няколко дни
seegoorno shteh seh opravite slet nyakolko dnee
it should clear up in a few days

сигурно ще заздравее бързо
seegoorno shteh zazdrave-eh burzo
it should heal quickly

ще ви напиша рецепта
shteh vee napeesha retsepta
I'm going to write you a prescription

AT THE CHEMIST'S

Expressing yourself

I'd like a box of plasters, please
една кутийка с лепенки, ако обичате
edna kooteeyka slepenki, ako obeechateh

could I have something for a bad cold?
моля, дайте ми нещо за тежка настинка
molya, dayteh mee neshto za teshka nasteenka

I need something for a cough
трябва ми нещо срещу кашлица
tryabva mee neshto sreshtoo kashlitsa

I'm allergic to aspirin
алергичен (m)/алергична (f) съм към аспирин
alergeechen/alergeechna sum kum aspireen

I need the morning-after pill
имам нужда от хапче срещу забременяване
eemam noozhda ot Hapcheh sreshtoo zabremenyavaneh

I'd like to try a homeopathic remedy
искам да опитам хомеопатично средство
eeskam da opeetam Home-opateechno sretstvo

I'd like a bottle of solution for soft contact lenses
дайте ми шише разтвор за контактни лещи
dayteh mee shisheh rastvor za kontaktni leshti

do you have a mosquito repellent?
имате ли лосион против комари?
eemateh lee losi-on proteef komari?

Understanding

възможни странични явления	possible side effects
външно	apply
да се взима три пъти на ден преди хранене	take three times a day before meals
капсула	capsule
крем	cream
противопоказания	contra-indications
пудра	powder
само по лекарско предписание	available on prescription only
свещички	suppositories
сироп	syrup
слънцезащитен крем	sun cream
таблетка	tablet
унгвент	ointment

Some informal expressions

имам ужасна хрема I have a stinking cold
пазя леглото I'm stuck in bed
скапан съм I feel rough

HEALTH

PROBLEMS AND EMERGENCIES

Members of the **KAT** (**Контрол по автотранспорта** *kontrol po aftotransporta*), known as **катаджии** *katadzhi-i*, are recognizable by their dark-grey uniforms and fluorescent green jackets: they control traffic and deal with road accidents (emergency number **165**). Members of the local and national police forces (**общинска полиция** *opshteenska poleetsi-ya* and **национална полиция** *natsi-onalna poleetsi-ya* respectively) wear dark-blue uniforms and are in charge of keeping order in towns. Members of the "gendarmerie" (**жандармерия** *zhandarmeri-ya*) are armed and deal with crimes committed outside of towns. Both types of police can be reached by dialling **166**. The border police (**гранична полиция** *graneechna poleetsi-ya*) deal with Customs matters. The number for the fire brigade is **160**; for medical emergencies (**бърза помощ** *burza pomosht*) dial **150**.

The basics

accident злополука *zlopolooka*
ambulance линейка *lineyka*, бърза помощ *burza pomosht*
broken счупен *schoopen*
coastguard брегова охрана *bregova oHrana*
disabled инвалид *invaleed*
doctor лекар *lekar*
emergency спешен случай *speshen sloochay*
fight бой *boy*
fire brigade пожарна (команда) *pozharna (komanda)*
fire пожар *pozhar*
hospital болница *bolnitsa*
ill болен (m)/болна (f) *bolen/bolna*
injured ранен (m)/ранена (f) *ranen/ranena*
late късно *kusno*

police полиция *poleetsi-ya*
policeman полицай *politsay*

Expressing yourself

can you help me?
можете ли да ми помогнете?
mozheteh lee da mee pomogneteh?

help!
помощ!
pomosht!

fire!
пожар!
pozhar!

be careful!
внимавай! *(sg)*/внимавайте! *(pl)*
vnimavay/vnimavayteh!

it's an emergency!
спешно е!
speshno eh!

could I borrow your phone, please?
бихте ли ми услужили с телефона си, моля?
beeHteh lee mee oosloozhili stelefona see, molya?

there's been an accident
стана злополука
stana zlopolooka

does anyone here speak English?
някой говори ли английски?
nyakoy govori lee angleeyski?

I need to contact the British consulate
трябва да се свържа с английското консулство
tryabva da seh svurzha sangleeyskoto konsoolstvo

where's the nearest police station?
къде е най-близкото полицейско управление?
kudeh eh nay-bleeskoto politseysko oopravleni-eh?

what do I have to do?
какво трябва да направя?
kakvo tryabva da napravya?

my passport/credit card has been stolen
откраднаха ми паспорта/кредитната карта
otkradnaHa mee pasporta/kreditnata karta

my bag's been snatched
взеха ми чантата
vzeHa mee chantata

I've lost …
изгубих …
izgoobiH …

I've been attacked
нападнаха ме
napadnaHa meh

my son/daughter is missing
синът ми/дъщеря ми изчезна
sinut mee/dushterya mee ischezna

my car's been towed away
вдигнаха колата ми
vdeegnaHa kolata mee

I've broken down
колата ми се развали
kolata mee seh razvalee

my car's been broken into
отваряли са колата ми
otvaryali sa kolata mee

there's a man following me
някой ме преследва
nyakoy meh presledva

is there disabled access?
има ли рампа/достъп за инвалиди?
eema lee rampa/dostup za invaleedi?

can you keep an eye on my things for a minute?
бихте ли наглеждали багажа ми за малко?
beeHteh lee naglezhdali bagazha mee za malko?

he's drowning, get help!
той се дави, извикайте помощ!
toy seh davi, izveekayteh pomosht!

Understanding

авар−ен изход	emergency exit
зло куче	beware of the dog
не работи	out of order
изгубени вещи	lost property
планинска спасителна служба	mountain rescue
пътна помощ	breakdown service
районно управление на МВР	local police station
свидетел	eyewitness
столична дирекция на МВР	the city of Sofia police department which also offers emergency services

POLICE

Expressing yourself

I want to report something stolen
искам да съобщя за кражба
eeskam da su-opshtyuh za krazhba

I need a document from the police for my insurance company
имам нужда от документ от полицията за застрахователната ми компания
eemam noozhda ot dokooment ot poleetsi-yata za zastraHovatelnata mee kompani-ya

Understanding

Filling in forms
адрес address
възраст age
дата на пристигане/отпътуване arrival/departure date
дата на раждане date of birth
дължина на престоя duration of stay
име first name
място на раждане place of birth
народност nationality
номер на паспорта passport number
пол sex
пощенски код postcode
професия/занятие occupation
страна country
фамилно име surname

бихте ли отворили чантата, ако обичате?
beeHteh lee otvorili chantata, ako obeechateh?
would you open this bag, please?

за този предмет се плаща мито
za tozi predmet seh plashta mito
there's Customs duty to pay on this item

какво липсва?
kakvo leepsva?
what's missing?

кога се случи това?
koga seh sloochi tova?
when did this happen?

къде сте отседнали?
kudeh steh otsednali?
where are you staying?

можете ли да го/я/го опишете?
mozheteh lee da go/ya/go opeesheteh?
can you describe him/her/it?

моля, подпишете тук
molya, potpisheteh took
would you sign here, please?

моля, попълнете този формуляр
molya, populneteh tozi formoolyar
would you fill in this form, please?

Some informal expressions

закопчаха го *zakopchaHa go* they put him behind bars
патрулка *patroolka* patrol car
свивам/да свия *sveevam/da svee-ya* to steal
ченге *chengeh* cop

Time expressions are quite different in the two languages. When talking about duration, for instance, you need to bear in mind whether you are referring to the past or the future because this will determine your choice of preposition. For instance, "we've been here for ten days" is rendered as тук сме от десет дена *took smeh ot deset dena* and "we're going to Varna for ten days" is заминаваме за Варна за десет дена *zaminavameh za varna za deset dena*. The duration sense does not usually require a preposition: "I waited for 15 minutes" is чаках петнайсет минути *chakaH petnayset minooti* and "I've been working in advertising for five years now" is работя в рекламата вече пет години *rabotya freklamata vecheh pet godeeni*. For longer periods or for emphasis you can use something like "throughout": for three centuries в продължение на три века *fprodulzheni-eh na tree veka*.

For what prepositions to use with which words see the lists below.

The basics

after след *slet*
already вече *vecheh*
all day цял ден *tsyal den*
all night цяла нощ *tsyala nosht*
all the time през цялото време *pres tsyaloto vremeh*
always винаги *veenagi*
at lunchtime по обед *po obet*
at night през нощта *prez noshta*
at the beginning/end of в началото/в края на *fnachaloto/fkra-ya na*
at the moment в момента *fmomenta*
before преди *predee*
between ... and ... между ... и ... *mezhdoo ... ee ...*
day ден *den*
during през *pres*
during the day през деня *prez denyuh*
early рано *rano*

evening вечер *vecher*
for a long time дълго *dulgo*
from ... to ... от ... до ... *ot ... do ...*
from time to time отвреме-навреме *otvremeh navremeh*
in a little while скоро *skoro*
in spring през пролетта *pres proleta*
in the evening вечерта *vecherta*
in the middle of в средата на *fsredata na*
in two days след два дни *slet dva dnee*
last последен *posleden*
late късно *kusno*
midday обед *obet*
midnight полунощ *poloonosht*
morning сутрин *sootrin*
month месец *mesets*
never никога *neekoga*
next следващият *sledvashti-yat*
night нощ *nosht*
not yet още не *oshteh neh*
now сега *sega*
occasionally понякога *ponyakoga*
often често *chesto*
rarely рядко *ryatko*
recently напоследък *naposleduk*
since от *ot*
sometimes понякога *ponyakoga*
soon скоро *skoro*
still още *oshteh*
straightaway веднага *vednaga*
until до *do*
week седмица *sedmitsa*
weekend края на седмицата *kra-ya na sedmitsata*, уикенд *oo-eekent*
year година *godeena*

Expressing yourself

see you soon!
до скоро
do skoro

see you later!
пак ще се видим
pak shteh seh veedim

see you on Monday!
ще се видим в понеделник
shteh seh veedim fponedelnik

have a good weekend!
приятен уикенд
pri-yaten oo-eekent

sorry I'm late
извинявайте, че закъснях
izvinyavayteh, cheh zakusnyaH

I haven't been there yet
още не съм ходил *(m)*/ходила *(f)* там
oshteh neh sum Hodil/Hodila tam

I haven't had time to …
нямах време да …
nyamaH vremeh da …

I've got plenty of time
имам много време
eemam mnogo vremeh

I'm in a rush
бързам
burzam

hurry up!
побързайте!
poburzayteh!

just a minute, please
една минута, моля
edna minoota, molya

I had a late night
снощи си легнах късно
snoshti see legnaH kusno

I got up very early
станах много рано
stanaH mnogo rano

I waited ages
чаках ужасно дълго
chakaH oozhasno dulgo

I have to get up very early tomorrow to catch my plane
трябва да стана много рано утре да хвана самолета
tryabva da stana mnogo rano ootreh da Hvana samoleta

we only have four days left
остават ни още четири дни
ostavat nee oshteh chetiri dnee

THE DATE

To say the date in Bulgarian you use the **ordinal** numbers (see pages 125-6) – the masculine for the day and the feminine for the year. A date written **2 January 1634** is literally expressed as "the second (*implied: day*

of) January (*implied: of*) one thousand six hundred and thirty-fourth year", втори (*m*) януари хиляда шестстотин трийсет и четвърта (*f*) година *ftori yanoo-ari Hilyada shestotin treeyset ee chetvurta godeena*. Even if the word година "year" isn't mentioned, it is always implied and the last digit remains in the feminine form. So: **in 2007**, literally expressed as "during 2007th", can be през две хиляди и седма *prez dveh Heelyadi ee sedma*. Similarly, **in November 1989** през ноември хиляда деветстотин осемдесет и девета (година) *prez no-emvri Hilyada devetstotin sheyset ee deveta (godeena)*. Centuries are written in Roman numerals: **in the 19th century** през XIX (деветнайсети) век *prez devetnaysti vek*.

The basics

... (days) ago преди ... дни *predee ... dnee*
at the beginning/end of в началото/в края на *fnachaloto na/fkra-ya na*
in the middle of в средата на *fsredata na*
in two days' time след два дни *sled dva dnee*
last night снощи *snoshti*
last week миналата седмица *meenalata sedmitsa*
next week следващата седмица *sledvashtata sedmitsa*
on 1 May на първи май *na purvi may*
on Wednesday в сряда *fsryada*
the day after tomorrow вдругиден *vdroogiden*
the day before yesterday оня ден *onya den*
today днес *dnes*
tomorrow утре *ootreh*
tomorrow morning/afternoon/evening утре сутринта/следобед/
вечерта *ootreh sootrinta/sledobet/vecherta*
until yesterday до вчера *do fchera*
yesterday morning/afternoon/evening вчера сутринта/следобед/
вечерта *fchera sootrinta/sledobet/vecherta*

Expressing yourself

I was born in 1975
роден (*m*)/родена (*f*) съм през хиляда деветстотин и седемдесет и
пета година
roden/rodena sum pres Hilyada devetstotin sedemdeset ee peta godeena

I came here a few years ago
дойдох тук преди няколко години
doydoH took predee nyakolko godeeni

I spent a month here last summer
прекарах тук един месец миналото лято
prekaraH took edeen mesets meenaloto lyato

I was here last year at the same time
бях тук по същото време миналата година
byaH took po sushtoto vremeh meenalata godeena

what's the date today?
коя дата е днес?
ko-ya data eh dnes?

what day is it today?
кой ден е днес?
koy den eh dnes?

it's the 1st of May
първи май е
purvi may eh

I'm staying until Sunday
тук съм до неделя
took sum do nedelya

we're leaving tomorrow
заминаваме утре
zaminavameh ootreh

I already have plans for Tuesday
вече имам планове за вторник
vecheh eemam planoveh za ftornik

Understanding

веднъж/два пъти once/twice
всеки ден every day
всеки понеделник every Monday
три пъти на час/на ден three times an hour/a day

кога заминавате?
koga zaminavateh?
when are you leaving?

за колко време сте тук?
za kolko vremeh steh took?
how long are you staying?

построен *(m)*/**построена** *(f)* е в средата на деветнайсети век
postro-en/postro-ena eh fsredata na devetnaysti vek
it was built in the mid-nineteenth century

през лятото тук идват много хора
prez lyatoto took eedvat mnogo Hora
it gets very busy here in the summer

THE TIME

On timetables, the 24-hour clock is used and the hour is followed by **ч.**, an abbreviation of the word for hour (**часа** *chasuh*). For example, 4pm is written **16 ч.** and 13:45 is written **13.45** or **13 ч. 45 мин.** (**минути** *minooti*).

In spoken language you use the 12-hour clock. For "am" you say **сутринта** *sootrinta* (in the morning) and for "pm" you say **следобед** *sledobet* (in the afternoon) or **вечерта** *vecherta* (in the evening).

To ask what time it is you say **колко е часът?** *kolko eh chasuh* (literally: "how much is the hour?"). To say that it's 3 o'clock, you would say **три часа** *tree chasuh*. Two important meanings of the word **час** "hour" are distinguished by stress only. When the stress is on the first syllable (*chasa*), it is a plural form and is used after numbers to express duration in hours: "I slept for three hours" **спах три часа** *spaH tree chasa*. When the stress is on the second syllable (*chasut/chasuh*) it is a singular but definite form and refers to times of the clock: "it's 5 o'clock" **часът е пет** *chasut e pet*, "come at 3am" **елате в три часа** *elateh ftree chasuh*.

Some informal expressions

бъди точен *(m)*/**точна** *(f) budee tochen/tochna* be on time
гледай да не закъснееш *gleday da neh zakusne-esh* don't be late
осем и нещо *osem ee neshto* it's just gone 8 o'clock
точно в два *tochno vdva* at 2 o'clock on the dot

The basics

about six hours около 6 часа *okolo shest chasa*
around 6 o'clock към шест часа *kum shest chasuh*
early рано *rano*
before lunch преди обед *predee obet*
half an hour половин час *poloveen chas*
in the afternoon следобед *sledobet*
in the morning сутринта *sootrinta*

late късно *kusno*
midday обед *obet*
midnight полунощ *poloonosht*
on time навреме *navremeh*
... (minutes) past 8 осем и ... (минути) *osem ee ... (minooti)*
quarter of an hour четвърт час *chetvurt chas*
three quarters of an hour 45 минути *cheteeriset ee pet minooti*
... (minutes) to 8 осем без ... (минути) *osem bez ... (minooti)*
until 12 o'clock до дванайсет часа *do dvanayset chasuh*

what time is it?
колко е часът?
kolko eh chasuh?

excuse me, have you got the time, please?
извинете, знаете ли колко е часът?
izvineteh, zna-eteh lee kolko eh chasuh?

it's exactly three o'clock
точно три часа е
tochno tree chasuh eh

it's nearly one o'clock
почти един часа е
pochtee edeen chasuh eh

it's ten past one
един и десет е
edeen ee deset eh

it's a quarter past one
един и петнайсет е
edeen ee petnayset eh

it's a quarter to one
един без петнайсет е
edeen bes petnayset eh

it's twenty past twelve
дванайсет и двайсет е
dvanayset ee dvayset eh

it's twenty to twelve
дванайсет без двайсет е
dvanayset bez dvayset eh

it's half past one
един и половина е
edeen ee poloveena eh

I arrived at about two o'clock
пристигнах към два часа
pristeegnaH kum dva chasuh

I set my alarm for nine
нагласих будилника за девет
naglaseeH boodeelnika za devet

I waited twenty minutes
чаках двайсет минути
chakaH dvayset minooti

the train was fifteen minutes late
влакът закъсня с двайсет минути
vlakut zakusnya zdvayset minooti

I got home an hour ago
върнах се вкъщи преди един час
vurnaH seh fkushti predee edeen chas

shall we meet in half an hour?
искате ли да се срещнем след половин час?
eeskateh lee da seh sreshnem slet poloveen chas

I'll be back in a quarter of an hour
ще се върна след петнайсет минути
shteh seh vurna slet petnayset minooti

there's a three-hour time difference between ... and ...
часовата разлика между ... и ... е три часа
chasovata razlika mezhdoo ... ee ... eh tree chasa

Understanding

отворено от 10 сутринта до 4 open from 10am to 4pm
следобед

тръгва в точен час и в и departs on the hour and the half-hour
половина

дават това шоу чуелй део пф уеден
davat tova sho-oo fseki den ot sedem
the show is on every evening at seven

отварят в десет сутринта   трае около час и половина
otvaryat vdeset sootrinta   *tra-eh okolo chas ee poloveena*
it opens at ten in the morning   it lasts around an hour and a half

Most numbers in Bulgarian agree with the gender of the items being counted. The **number 1** has three forms: **един билет** *edeen bilet* one ticket (masculine), **една жена** *edna zhena* one woman (feminine), **едно дете** *edno deteh* one child (neuter). The **number 2** has only two forms: **два** *dva* for the masculine and **две** *dveh* for the feminine and neuter. So you would say **два билета** *dva bileta* two tickets, and **две жени/деца** *dveh zhenee/detsa* two women/children. Compound numbers ending with 1 and 2 must also agree with the noun: **двайсет и една жени** *dvayset ee edna zhenee* 21 women, **двайсет и две деца** *dvayset ee dveh detsa* 22 children.

In the list below, only the neuter form of 1 and 2 is given as that is the one used for counting. When counting between 2 and 6 people (with at least one male among them), the suffix **-ма** *-ma* (or **-има** *-ima* after a consonant) is added to the number: **двама мъже** *dvama muzheh* two men, **петима лекари** *peteema lekari* five doctors. When counting people in general (**души** *dooshi* or **човека** *choveka*), the number with the **-ма/-има** suffix is used again: **четирима души** *chetireema dooshi* four people.

There are two ways to write numbers from **11 upwards**: a long form (**единадесет** *edinadeset* eleven, **дванадесет** *dvanadeset* twelve etc, literally "one/two above ten") and a short form (**единайсет** *edinayset*, **дванайсет** *dvanayset* …). The second form is almost always used in speech and there is a further simplification as the final t is dropped. In the list below we have given only the short form with potentially dropped sounds in brackets (except for the numbers 50, 70, 80 and 90, which only have a long form).

All **ordinal** numbers (first, second etc) agree with the gender of the noun (ending in **-и** *-i* in the masculine, **-а** *-a* in the feminine and **-о** *-o* in the neuter). For example, "first" is **първи** *purvi* (or **пръв** *pruf*) (masculine), **първа** *purva* (feminine) or **първо** *purvo* (neuter); "second" is **втори** *ftori* (masculine), **втора** *ftora* (feminine), **второ** *ftoro* (neuter). In the following list, we give only the masculine form. In the plural, the word ends in **-и** *-i* for all three genders: **първи** first (plural), **втори** second (plural). If you

want to add an article, it goes on the end of the ordinal number: **първият** (masculine), **първата** (feminine), **първото** (neuter), **първите** (plural) the first. Ordinal numbers are often written as Roman numerals.

0 нула *noola*
1 едно *edno*
2 две *dveh*
3 три *tree*
4 четири *chet(i)ri*
5 пет *pet*
6 шест *shes(t)*
7 седем *sedem*
8 осем *osem*
9 девет *devet*
10 десет *deset*
11 единайсет *edinayse(t)*
12 дванайсет *dvanayse(t)*
13 тринайсет *trinayse(t)*
14 четиринайсет *chet(i)rinayse(t)*
15 петнайсет *petnayse(t)*
16 шестнайсет *shes(t)nayse(t)*
17 седемнайсет *sedemnayse(t)*
18 осемнайсет *osemnayse(t)*
19 деветнайсет *devetnayse(t)*
20 двайсет *dvayse(t)*
21 двайсет и едно *dvayse(t) ee edno*
22 двайсет и две *dvayse(t) ee dveh*
30 трийсет *treeyse(t)*
35 трийсет и пет *treeyse(t) ee pet*
40 четиресет *cheteerise(t)*
50 петдесет *pe(t)dese(t)*
60 шестдесет *sheyse(t)*
70 седемдесет *sedemdese(t)*
80 осемдесет *osemdese(t)*
90 деветдесет *deve(t)dese(t)*
100 сто *sto*
101 сто и едно *sto ee edno*
200 двеста *dvesta*
300 триста *treesta*
400 четиристотин *chetiristotin*
500 петстотин *petstotin*
1000 хиляда *Hilyada*
2000 две хиляди *dveh Hilyadi*
10000 десет хиляди *deset Hilyadi*
1000000 един милион *edeen mili-on*

first първи, първа, първо, първи
purvi, purva, purvo, purvi
second втори, втора, второ, втори
ftori, ftora, ftoro, ftori
third трети *treti*
fourth четвърти *chetvurti*
fifth пети *peti*
sixth шести *shesti*
seventh седми *sedmi*
eighth осми *osmi*
ninth девети *deveti*
tenth десети *deseti*
twentieth двайсети *dvays(e)ti*

20 plus 3 equals 23
двайсет плюс три прави двайсет
и три
dvayset plyus tree pravi dvayset ee tree

20 minus 3 equals 17
двайсет минус три прави
седемнайсет
dvayset meenus tree pravi sedemnayset

20 multiplied by 4 equals 80
двайсет по четири прави осемдесет
dvayset po chetiri pravi osemdeset

20 divided by 4 equals 5
двайсет делено на четири прави
пет
dvayset deleno na chetiri pravi pet

NUMBERS

DICTIONARY

ENGLISH-BULGARIAN

Adjectives are given in their masculine form. For the other forms consult the Grammar section (pages 176–7). Verbs are listed with both imperfective and perfective variant, the latter accompanied by **да** as a reminder that in the present tense perfective variants can't be used on their own.

A

a един *edeen*
able: to be able to мога *moga*
about за *za*; около *okolo*; към *kum*; **to be about to do** скоро ще ... *skoro shteh* ...
above горе *goreh*
abroad в чужбина *fchoozhbeena*
accent акцент *aktsent*
accept приемам/да приема *pri-emam/da pri-ema*
access достъп *dostup* 114
accident злополука *zlopolooka*; катастрофа *katastrofa* 34, 113
accommodation квартира *kvarteera*
account сметка *smetka*
across през *pres*
adaptor адаптор *adaptor*
address адрес *adres* 21
admission вход *fHot*
advance: in advance предварително *predvareetelno*
advice съвет *suvet*; **to ask someone's advice** искам съвет от някого *eeskam suvet ot nyakogo*
advise съветвам *suvetvam*
aeroplane самолет *samolet*
after след *slet*
afternoon следобед *sledobet*
after-sun (cream) (крем) за след излагане на слънце *(krem) za slet izlaganeh na sluntseh*
again пак *pak*
against срещу *sreshtoo*
age възраст *vuzrast*; **for ages** много дълго *mnogo dulgo*

air въздух *vuzdooH*
air conditioning климатик *klimateek*
airline авиокомпания *avi-okompani-ya*
airmail въздушна поща *vuzdooshna poshta*
airport летище *leteeshteh*, аерогара *a-erogara*
alarm аларма *alarma*
alarm clock будилник *boodeelnik*
alcohol алкохол *alkoHol*
alive жив *zhif*
all всички *fseechki*; **all day** цял ден *tsyal den*; **all week** цяла седмица *tsyala sedmitsa*; **all the better** още-по добре *oshteh po-dobreh*; **all the same** все едно *fseh edno*; **all the time** през цялото време *pres tsyaloto vremeh*; **all inclusive** включително *fklyucheetelno*
allergic алергичен *alergeechen* 49, 108, 110
almost почти *pochtee*
already вече *vecheh*
also също *sushto*
although въпреки че *vupreki cheh*
always винаги *veenagi*
ambulance линейка *lineyka* 106
American (noun) американец *amerikanets*, американка *amerikanka*
American (adj) американски *amerikanski*
among сред *sret*
amount сума *sooma*
anaesthetic упойка *ooroyka*
and и *ee*
animal животно *zhivotno*
ankle глезен *glezen*
anniversary годишнина *godeeshnina*
another друг *drook*

answer (noun) отговор otgovor
answer (v) отговарям/да отговоря otgovaryam/da otgovorya
answering machine телефонен секретар telefonen sekretar
ant мравка mrafka
antibiotics антибиотик antibi-otik
anybody, anyone някой nyakoy
anything нещо neshto
anyway както и да е kakto ee da eh
apartment апартамент apartament
appendicitis апендисит apendiseet
appointment среща sreshta; **to make an appointment** запазвам час zapazvam chas 106; **to have an appointment (with)** имам среща с eemam sreshta s 106
April април apreel
area район ray-on, зона zona; **in the area** в този район ftozi ray-on
arm ръка ruka
around (на) около (na)okolo
arrange уговарям/да уговоря oogovaryam/ da oogovorya; **to arrange to meet** уговарям среща с oogovaryam sreshta s
arrival пристигане pristeeganeh
arrive пристигам/да пристигна pristeegam/da pristeegna
art изкуство iskoostvo
artist художник (m) Hoodozhnik, художничка (f) Hoodozhnichka
as като kato; **as soon as possible** колкото може по-бързо kolkoto mozheh po-burzo; **as soon as** щом като shtom kato; **as well as** също и sushto ee
ashtray пепелник pepelneek 47
ask питам/да попитам peetam/da popeetam; **to ask a question** задавам/да задам въпрос zadavam/da zadam vupros
aspirin аспирин aspireen
asthma астма astma
at в/във v/vuf
attack (v) нападам/да нападна napadam/da napadna
attention внимание vnimani-eh
August август avgoost
autumn есен esen
available: to be available има eema; **not to be available** няма nyama
away: 10 miles away на десет мили от na deset meeli ot

B

baby бебе bebeh
baby's bottle бебешко шише bebeshko shisheh
back гръб grup; **at the back of** на гърба на na gurbuh na
backpack раница ranitsa
bad лош losh; **it's not bad** не е лошо neh eh losho
bag чанта chanta; **plastic bag** плик pleek, торбичка torbeechka
baggage багаж bagash
bake пека/да изпека pekuh/da ispekuh
baker's хлебарница Hlebarnitsa
balcony балкон balkon
band оркестър orkestur, група groopa
bandage превръзка prevruska
bank банка banka 92
banknote банкнота banknota
bar бар bar
barbecue барбекю barbekyu, грил greel, скара skara
basic основен osnoven
bath вана vana; **to have a bath** къпя се/да се окъпя kupya seh/da seh okupya
bath towel хавлиена кърпа Havlee-ena kurpa
bathroom баня banya
battery (car) акумулатор akoomoolator; батерия bateri-ya 34
be съм sum
beach плаж plash
beach umbrella чадър chadur
beard брада brada
beautiful красив kraseef
because защото zashtoto; **because of** поради poradee
bed легло leglo
bee пчела pchela
before преди predee
begin започвам/да започна zapochvam/ da zapochna
beginner начинаещ nachina-esht
beginning начало nachalo; **at the beginning** в началото fnachaloto
behind зад zat
believe вярвам/да повярвам vyarvam/da povyarvam
below отдолу otdoloo

beside до *do*; освен *osven*

best най-добър *nay-dobur*; **the best** най-добрият *nay-dobreeyat*

better по-добър *po-dobur*; **to get better** оздравявам *ozdravyavam*; **it's better to...** по-добре да *...po-dobreh da...*

between между *mezhdoo*

bicycle велосипед *velosipet*, колело *kolelo*

bicycle pump помпа за велосипед *pompa za velosipet*

big голям *golyam*

bike колело *kolelo*

bill сметка *smetka* 51

bin кошче *koshcheh*

binoculars бинокъл *binokul*

birthday рожден ден *rozhden den*

bit парче *parcheh*

bite (*v*) ухапване *ooHapvaneh*

bite (*v*) хапя/да ухапя *hapya/da ooHapya*

black черен *cheren*

blackout загуба на съзнание *zagooba na suznani-eh*, причерняване *prichernyavaneh*

blanket одеало *ode-alo*

bleed: it's bleeding тече кръв *techeh kruf*; **I'm bleeding** тече ми кръв *techeh mee kruf*

bless: bless you! наздраве *nazdraveh*; благодаря, да си жив и здрав *blagodaryuh, da see zheef ee zdraf*

blind сляп *slyap*

blister пришка *preeshka*

blocked блокиран *blokeeran*; блокирал *blokeeral*

blood кръв *kruf*

blood pressure кръвно налягане *kruvno nalyaganeh*

blue син *seen*

board дъска *duska* 28

boarding качване *kachvaneh*

boat кораб *korap*; **fishing boat** лодка *lotka*

body тяло *tyalo*

book (*noun*) книга *kneega*

book (*v*) запазвам/да запазя *zapazvam/da zapazya*

bookshop книжарница *knizharnitsa*

boot висока обувка *visoka oboofka*, ботуш *botoosh*; (*of car*) багажник *bagazhnik*

born роден (*m*) /родена (*f*) *roden/rodena*

borrow вземам назаем/да взема назаем *vzemam naza-em/da vzema naza-em*

botanical garden ботаническа градина *botaneecheska gradeena*

both и двата (*m*) ee *dvata*/и двете ee *dveteh* (*f*); **both of us** и двамата (*m*) ee *dvamata* /и двете ee *dveteh* (*f*)

bottle бутилка *booteelka*

bottle opener отварячка *otvaryachka*

bottom дъно *duno*; **at the bottom** на дъното *na dunoto*; **at the bottom of** на дъното на *a dunoto na*

bowl купа *koopa*

box кутия *kootee-ya*; **telephone box** телефонна кабина *telefonna kabeena*

boy момче *momcheh*

boyfriend приятел *pree-yatel*

bra сутиен *sooti-en*

brake (*noun*) спирачка *spirachka*

brake (*v*) спирам/да спра *speeram/da spruh*

bread хляб *Hlyap*; **bread roll** питка *peetka*

break чупя/да счупя *choopya/da schoopya*; **to break one's leg** да си счупя крака *da se schoopya krakuh*

break down закъсвам/да закъсам *zakusvam/da zakusam* 34

breakdown повреда *povreda*

breakdown service пътна помощ *putna pomosht*

breakfast закуска *zakooska* 40; **to have breakfast** закусвам/да закуся *zakoosvam/da zakoosya*

bridge мост *most*

bring нося/да донеса *nosya/da donesuh*

brochure брошура *broshoora*

broken счупен *schoopen*

bronchitis бронхит *bronHeet*

brother брат *brat*

brown кафяв *kafyaf*

brush четка *chetka*

build строя/да построя *stro-ya/da postro-ya*

building сграда *zgrada*

bumper броня *bronya*

buoy шамандура *shamandoora*

burn (*noun*) изгаряне *izgaryaneh*

burn (*v*) изгарям/да изгоря *izgaryam/da*

izgoryuh; **to burn oneself** изгарям се/да се изгоря *izgaryam seh/da seh izgoryuh*

burst (v) пукам/да спукам *pookam/da spookam*

burst (adj) спукан *spookan*

bus автобус *aftoboos*

bus route маршрут *marshroot*

bus station автогара *aftogara*

bus stop автобусна спирка *aftoboosna speerka*

busy зает *za-et*; оживен *ozhiven*, претъпкан *pretupkan*

but но *no*

butcher's месарница *mesarnitsa*

buy купувам/да купя *koopoovam/da koopya*

by с/със *s/sus*; **by car** с кола *skola* **by the doctor** от лекаря *ot lekarya*

bye! чао *cha-o*

C

cable television кабелна телевизия *kabelna televeezi-ya*

café кафене *kafeneh*

call (noun) обаждане *obazhdaneh*; разговор *razgovor*

call (v) обаждам се/да се обадя *obazhdam seh/da seh obadya* **103**; **to be called** казвам се *kazvam seh*

call back обаждам се *obazhdam seh* **103**

camera фотоапарат *fotoaparat*

camper къмпингар *kumpingar*

camping къмпингуване *kumpingoovaneh*; **to go camping** ходя на къмпинг *Hodya na kumpink*

camping stove къмпингов котлон *kumpingof kotlon*

campsite къмпинг *kumpink* **44**

can (noun) консерва *konserva*

can (v) мога *moga*; **I can't** не мога *neh moga*

can opener отварячка за консерви *otvaryachka za konservi*

cancel отменям/да отменя *otmenyam/da otmenya*, анулирам *anooleeram*

candle свещ *svesht*

car кола *kola*

car park паркинг *parkink*

caravan каравана *karavana*

card карта *karta*; (visiting) картичка *kartichka*; **identity card** лична карта *leechna karta* **top-up card** ваучер *va-oocher*, предплатена карта *pretplatena karta*

carry нося *nosya*

case: in case of... в случай на... *fsloochay na...*

cash в брой *vbroy*; **to pay cash** плащам в брой/да платя в брой *plashtam vbroy/da platyuh vbroy*

cashpoint банкомат *bankomat* **92**

castle замък *zamuk*

catch хващам/да хвана *Hvashtam/da Hvana*

cathedral катедрала *katedrala*

CD сиди *seedee*, компактдиск *kompaktdisk*

celebration празненство *praznenstvo*

cemetery гробища *grobishta*

centimetre сантиметър *santimetur*

centre център *tsentur*

century век *vek*

chair стол *stol*

chairlift открит лифт *otkreet leeft*

chance възможност *vuzmozhnost*; **by chance** случайно *sloochayno*

change (noun) промяна *promyana*; (money) дребни пари *drebni paree*; ресто *resto* **83**; **bureau de change** обменно бюро *obmenno byuro*

change (v) сменям/да сменя *smenyam/da smenyuh*; (money) обменям/да обменя *obmenyam/da obmenyuh* **92**; **to change transport** прехвърлям се/да се прехвърля *preHvurlyam seh/da seh preHvurlya*, прекачвам се/да се прекача *prekachvam seh/da seh prekachuh*

changing room съблекалня *sublekalnya*, пробна *probna* **85**

channel канал *kanal*

chapel параклис *paraklis*

charge (noun) такса *taksa*, комисионна *komisi-onna*

charge (v) (money) вземам/да взема пари *vzemam/da vzema paree*; (telephone) зареждам/да заредя *zarezhdam/da zaredyuh*

cheap евтин *eftin*

check проверявам/да проверя *proveryavam/da proveryuh*

check in регистрирам се *registreeram seh*
check-in регистрация *registratsi-ya* **28**
check out напускам/да напусна
napooskam/da napoosna
cheers! наздраве *nazdraveh*
chemist's аптека *apteka*
cheque чек *chek*
chest гърди *gurdee*
child дете *deteh*; **children** деца *detsa*
chilly хладен *Hladen*
chimney комин *komeen*
chin брадичка *bradeechka*
church църква *tsurkva*
cigar пура *poora*
cigarette цигара *tsigara*
cigarette paper листчета за цигари
leestcheta za tsigari
cinema кино *keeno*
circus цирк *tseerk*
city град *grat*
clean (adj) чист *cheest*
clean (v) чистя/да изчистя *cheestya/da
ischeestya*
cliff скала *skala*
climate климат *kleemat*
climbing катерене *katereneh*, качване
kachvaneh, туризъм *tooreezwm*
cloakroom гардероб *garderop*
close (v) затварям/да затворя *zatvaryam/
da zatvorya*
closed затворено *zatvoreno*
closing time край на работното време
kray na rabotnoto vremeh
clothes дрехи *dreHi*
club клуб *kloop*
clutch съединител *su-edineetel*
coach автобус *aftoboos*
coast бряг *bryak*
coathanger закачалка *zakachalka*
cockroach хлебарка *Hlebarka*
code код *kot*
coffee кафе *kafeh*
coil (contraceptive) спирала *spirala*
coin монета *moneta*
Coke® кола *kola*
cold (noun) настинка *nasteenka*; хрема
Hrema; **to have a cold** настинал (m)/
настинала (f) съм *nasteenal/nasteenala sum*
cold (adj) студен *stooden*; **it's cold**
студено е *stoodeno eh*; **I'm cold**
студено ми е *stoodeno mee eh*

collection колекция *kolektsee-ya*
colour цвят *tsvyat*; **colour photo** цветна
снимка *tsvetna sneemka*
comb гребен *greben*
come идвам/да дойда *eedvam/da doyda*;
come! ела (sing)/елате (pl) ela, *elateh*
come back връщам се/да се върна
vrushtam seh/da seh vurna
come in влизам/да вляза *vleezam/da
vlyaza*
come out излизам/да изляза *izleezam/
da izlyaza*
comfortable удобен *oodoben*
company компания *kompani-ya*
compartment купе *koopeh*
complain оплаквам се/да се оплача
oplakvam seh/da seh oplacha
comprehensive insurance пълна
застраховка *pulna zastraHofka*; (car)
автокаско *aftokasko* **34**
computer компютър *kompyutur*
concert концерт *kontsert*
concert hall концертна зала *kontsertna
zala*
concession намаление *namaleni-eh*
26, 71
condition (medical) заболяване
zabolyavaneh
condom презерватив *prezervateef*
confirm потвърждавам/да потвърдя
potvurzhdavam/da potvurdyuh **28**
connection връзка *vruska* **28**
constipated запечен *zapechen*
consulate консулство *konsoolstvo* **113**
contact (noun) контакт *kontakt*
contact (v) свързвам се с/да се свържа
svurzvam seh s/da seh svurzha s; обаждам
се/да се обадя *obazhdam seh/da seh
obadya* **102, 113**
contact lenses контактни лещи
kontaktni leshti
contagious заразен *zarazen*
contraceptive противозачатъчно
protivozachatuchno
cook готвя/да сготвя *gotvya/da zgotvya*
cooked сготвен *zgotven*
cooking готвене *gotveneh*; **to do the
cooking** готвя *gotvya*
cool прохладен *proHladen*; готин *gotin*
copy (noun) копие *kopi-eh*
copy (v) копирам *kopeeram*

corkscrew тирбушон *tirbooshon*

corner ъгъл *ugul*

correct правилен *pravilen*

cost (v) струвам *stroovam*

cottage (селска) къща *(selska) kushta*

cotton: made of cotton памучен *pamoochen*; **cotton wad** памучна клечка *pamoochna klechka*

cotton wool памук *pamook*

cough (noun) кашлица *kashlitsa*; **to have a cough** имам кашлица *eemam kashlitsa*

cough (v) кашлям *kashlyam*

count броя *bro-ya*

country страна *strana*

countryside природата извън града *prirodata izvun graduh*

course: of course разбира се *razbeera seh*

cover (noun) капак *kapak*

cover (v) покривам/да покрия *pokreevam/ da pokree-ya*

credit card кредитна карта *kreditna karta* **38, 51**

cross (noun) кръст *krust*

cross (v) пресичам *preseecham*

cruise круиз *kroo-eez*

cry плача *placha*

cup чаша *chasha*

currency валута *valoota*

customs митница *meetnitsa*

cut режа/да нарежа *rezha/da narezha*; **to cut oneself** порязвам се/да се порежа *poryazvam seh/da seh porezha*; **to cut off** прекъсвам/да прекъсна *prekusvam/da prekusna*

cycle path алея за велосипедисти *ale- ya za velosipedeesti*

D

damaged повреден *povreden*

damp влажен *vlazhen*

dance (noun) танц *tants*

dance (v) танцувам *tantsoovam*

danger опасност *opanost*; **danger!** внимание! *vnimani-eh*

dangerous опасен *opasen*

dark тъмен *tumen*; **dark blue** тъмносин *tumnoseen*

date (noun) дата *data*; **out of date** старомоден *staromoden*

date (from) датира от *dateera ot*

date of birth дата на раждане *data na razhdeneh*

daughter дъщеря *dushterya*

day ден *den*; **the day after tomorrow** вдругиден *vdroogiden*; **the day before yesterday** оня ден *onya den*

dead умрял *oomryal*

deaf глух *glooH*

dear скъп *skup*

debit card дебитна карта *debitna karta*

December декември *dekemvri*

declare декларирам *deklareeram*

deep дълбок *dulbok*

degree степен *stepen*; *(temperature)* градус *gradoos*

delay закъснение *zakusneni-eh*

delayed със закъснение *sus zakusneni- eh*

dentist зъболекар *zubolekar*

deodorant дезодорант *dezodorant*

depart тръгвам/да тръгна *trugvam/ da trugna*; заминавам/да замина *zaminavam/da zameena*

department отделение *otdeleni-eh*

department store универсален магазин *ooniversalen magazeen*

departure заминаване *zaminaveneh*

depend: that depends (on) зависи (от) *zaveesi (ot)*

deposit депозит *depozit*

dessert десерт *desert* **49**

destination дестинация *destinatsi-ya*

develop: to get a film developed да ми проявят филма *da mee proyavyut feelma* **89**

diabetes диабет *di-abet*

dial набирам/да набера *nabeeram/da naberuh*

dialling code код за избиране *kot za izbeeraneh*

diarrhoea: to have diarrhoea имам диария *eemam di-ari-ya*

die умирам *oomeeram*

diesel дизел *deezel*

diet режим на хранене *rezheem na Hraneneh*; **to be on a diet** на диета съм *na di-eta sum*

difference разлика *razlika*

different (from) различен от *razleechen ot*

difficult труден *trooden*

digital camera цифров фотоапарат *tseefrof foto-aparat*

dinner обед *obet*; **to have dinner** обядвам *obyadvam*

direct директен *direkten*, пряк *pryak*

direction посока *posoka*; **to have a good sense of direction** ориентирам се добре *ori-enteeram seh dobreh*

directory указател *ookazatel*

directory enquiries телефонни услуги *telefonni oosloogi*

dirty (adj) мръсен *mrusen*

disabled инвалид *invaleed*

disaster бедствие *betsvi-eh*; катастрофа *katastrofa*

disco дискотека *diskoteka*

discount намаление *namaleni-eh* **70**; **to give someone a discount** правя отстъпка *pravya otstupka*

discount fare с намаление *snamaleni-eh*

dish ястие *yasti-eh*; **dish of the day** специалитет на деня *spetsi-alitet na denyuh*

dishes чинии *chinee-i*; **to do the dishes** мия чиниите/да измия чиниите *mee-ya chinee-ite/da izmee-ya chinee-ite*

dish towel кърпа *kurpa*

dishwasher миялна машина *mi-yalna masheena*

disinfect дезинфекцирам *dezinfektseeram*

disposable за еднократна употреба *za ednokratna oopotreba*

disturb безпокоя *bespokoyuh*; **do not disturb** не ме безпокойте *neh meh bespokoyteh*

dive гмуркам се *gmoorkam seh*

diving подводен спорт *podvoden sport*

do правя/да направя *pravya/da napravya*; **do you have a light?** имате ли огън(че)? *eemateh lee ogun(cheh)?*

doctor лекар *lekar* **106**

door врата *vrata*

door code код за влизане *kot za vleezaneh*

double двоен *dvo-en*

downstairs на долния етаж *na dolni-ya etash*

draught beer наливна бира *naleevna beera*

dress: to get dressed обличам се/да се облека *obleecham seh/da seh oblekuh*

dressing сос *sos*, заливка *zaleefka*; подправка за салата *potprafka za salata*

drink (noun) напитка *napeetka*; **to go for a drink** отивам да пийна нещо *oteevam da peeyna neshto* **47, 62**; **to have a drink** пия/да изпия *pee-ya/da ispee-ya*

drink (v) пия/да изпия *pee-ya/da ispee-ya*

drinking water вода за пиене *voda za pee-eneh*

drive: (noun) to go for a drive отивам/да отида да покарам *oteevam/da oteeda da pokaram*

drive (v) карам *karam*

driving licence шофьорска книжка *shofyorska kneeshka*

drops капки *kapki*

drown давя се/да се удавя *davya seh/da seh oodavya*

drugs лекарства *lekarstva*; (addictive) наркотици *narkoteetsi*

drunk пиян *pi-yan*

dry (adj) сух *sooH*

dry (v) изсушавам/да изсуша *issooshavam/da issooshuh*

dry cleaner's химическо чистене *Himeechesko cheesteneh*

during през *pres*; **during the weekend** през уикенда *pres weekenda*

dustbin кошче за боклук *koshcheh za boklook*

duty chemist's дежурна аптека *dezhoorna apteka*

E

each всеки *fseki* (m), всяка *fsyaka* (f), всяко *fsyako* (noun); **each one** всеки *fseki*

ear ухо *ooHo*

early рано *rano*

earplugs тапи за уши *tapi za ooshee*

earrings обеци *obetsee*

earth земя *zemya*

east изток *eestok*; **in the east** на изток *na eestok*; **(to the) east of** на изток от *na eestok ot*

Easter Великден *veleekden*

easy лесен *lesen*

eat ям *yam* **47**; **to eat out** ходя на ресторант *Hodya na restorant*

economy class туристическа класа *tooriste*e*chka klasa*

Elastoplast® еластична лепенка *elaste*e*chna lepenka*

elderly възрастен *v*u*zrasten*

electric електрически *elektr*e*echeski*

electric shaver електрическа самобръсначка *elektr*e*echeska samobrusn*a*chka*

electricity електричество *elektr*e*echestvo*

electricity meter електромер *elektrom*e*r*

e-mail имейл *e*e*meyl*, електронна поща *elektr*o*nna poshta*

e-mail address имейл адрес *e*e*meyl adres* **21, 98**

embassy посолство *pos*o*lstvo*

emergency спешен случай *speshen sl*o*ochay*; **in an emergency** в случай на авария *fsl*o*ochay na avari-ya*

emergency exit аварен изход *avaree-en ees*H*ot*

empty празен *pr*a*zen*

end край *kray*; **at the end of** в края на *fkr*a*ya na*; **at the end of the street** в дъното на улицата *vd*u*noto na *o*olitsata*

engaged заето *za-*e*to*

engine мотор *mot*o*r*

England Англия *angli-ya*

English (n) англичанин *anglich*a*nin* (m), англичанка (f) *anglich*a*nka*

English (adj) английски *angle*e*yski*

enjoy: enjoy your meal! добър апетит! *dob*u*r apet*e*et*; **I'm enjoying myself** забавно ми е *zab*a*vno mee eh*

enough достатъчно *dost*a*tuchno*; **that's enough** стига *st*e*ega*

enquiries справки *spr*a*fki*; **directory enquiries** телефонни услуги *telef*o*nni oosl*o*ogi*

enter въвеждам/да въведа *vuv*e*zhdam/ da vuv*e*duh*

entrance вход *f*H*ot*

entry (fee) куверт *koov*e*rt*, входна такса *f*H*odna taksa*

envelope плик *pleek*

epileptic епилептик *epileept*e*ek* (m), епилептичка *epileepte*e*chka* (f)

equipment оборудване *oboro*o*dvaneh*

espresso еспресо *espr*e*so*

euro евро *evro*

Eurocheque еврочек *evrochek*

Europe Европа *evropa*

European европейски *evrop*e*yski*

evening вечер *vecher*; **in the evening** вечерта *vecher*t*a*

every всеки *fseki* (m), всяка *fsyaka* (f), всяко *fsyako* (noun); **every day** всеки ден *fseki den*

everybody, **everyone** всеки *fseki*

everywhere навсякъде *nafsyakudeh*

exact точен *t*o*chen*

except освен *osven*

exceptional изключителен *i*s*klyuchee*t*elen*

excess (luggage) свръх *svruH*, над лимита *nat limeeta*

exchange обмяна *obmyana*

exchange rate курс *koors*

excuse (noun) извинение *izvineni-eh*

excuse (v): **excuse me** извинявай *izvin*ya*vay* (sing) извинявайте *izvin*ya*vayteh* (pl)

exhaust изморявам *izmor*ya*vam*

exhausted изморен *izmoren*

exhaust pipe ауспух *a-oosp*oo*H*

exhibition изложба *izl*o*zhba* **70**

exit изход *eesHot*

expensive скъп *skup*

expiry date срок на годност *srok na g*o*dnost*

express (adj) експресен *ekspr*e*sen*

express (v) изразявам/да изразя *izraz*ya*vam/da izraz*y*uh*; **to express oneself** изразявам се/да се изразя *izraz*ya*vam seh/da seh izraz*y*uh*

extra допълнителен *dop*u*ln*ee*telen*, извънреден *izv*u*nreden*

eye око *oko*

F

face лице *litseh*

fact факт *fakt*; **in fact** всъщност *fs*u*shnost*

faint припадам/да припадна *prip*a*dam/ da pr*ee*padna*

fair (noun) панаир *pana-eer*

fall (v) падам/да падна *padam/da padna*; **to fall asleep** заспивам/да заспя *zasp*e*evam/da zasp*y*uh*; **to fall**

ill разболявам се/да се разболея *razbolyavam seh/da seh razbole-ya*

family семейство *semeystvo*

fan любител *lyubeetel*, фен *fen*

far далече *dalecheh*; **far from** далече от *dalecheh ot*

fare цена (на билет) *tsena (na bilet)*

fast бърз *burs*

fast-food restaurant ресторант за бърза закуска *restorant za burza zakooska*

fat мазнина *maznina*

father баща *bashta*

favour услуга *ooslooga*; **to do someone a favour** правя услуга на някого *pravya ooslooga na nyakogo*

favourite любим *lyubeem*

fax факс *faks*

February февруари *fevroo-ari*

fed up: to be fed up (with) омръзна (ми) *omruzna (mee)*

feel чувствам *choostvam*; **to feel good/bad** приятно ми е/не ми е приятно *pri-yatno mee eh/neh mee eh pri-yatno* **107**

feeling чувство *choostvo*

festival фестивал *festival*

fetch: to go and fetch someone да отида да доведа някого *da oteeda da doveduh nyakogo*; **to go and fetch something** да отида да донеса нещо *da oteeda da donesuh neshto*

fever висока температура *visoka temperatoora*; **to have a fever** имам висока температура *eemam visoka temperatoora*

few малко *malko*

fiancé годеник *godeneek*

fiancée годеница *godeneetsa*

fight кавга *kavga*

fill пълня/да напълня *pulnya/da napulnya*

fill in попълвам/да попълня *populvam/da populnya*

fill out изпълвам/да изпълня *ispulvam/da ispulnya*

fill up: to fill up with petrol напълвам/да напълня *napulvam/da napulnya*

filling (in tooth) пломба *plomba*

film (for camera) филм *feelm*; (movie) филм *feelm* **89**

final последен *posleden*

finally най-накрая *nay-nakraya*

find намирам/да намеря *nameeram/da namerya*

fine (noun) глоба *globa*

fine (adv) добре *dobreh*; **I'm fine** добре съм *dobreh sum*

finger пръст *prust*

finish свършвам/да свърша *svurshvam/da svursha*

fire огън *ogun*; **fire!** пожар! *pozhar*

fire brigade пожарна команда *pozharna komanda*

fireworks фойерверки *fo-yerverki*

first първи *purvi*; **first (of all)** първо *purvo*

first class първа класа *purva klasa*

first floor първи етаж *purvi etash*

first name име *eemeh*

fish (noun) риба *reeba*; **fish shop/restaurant** рибен магазин/ресторант *reeben magazeen/restorant*

fishmonger's рибен магазин *reeben magazeen*

fitting room пробна *probna*

fizzy газиран *gazeeran*

flash светкавица *svetkavitsa*

flask термос *termos*

flat (adj) плосък *plosuk*; **flat tyre** спукана гума *spookana gooma*

flat (noun) апартамент *apartament*

flavour вкус *fkoos*

flaw дефект *defekt*

flight полет *polet*

flip-flops джапанки *dzhapanki*

floor етаж *etash*; **on the floor** на пода *na poda*

flu грип *greep*

fly (noun) муха *mooHa*

fly (v) летя *letyua*

folk dancing народни танци *narodni tantsi*

food храна *Hrana*

food poisoning хранително отравяне *Hraneetelno otravyaneh*

foot крак *krak*; **on foot** пеша *pesha*

for за *za*; **for an hour** за един час *za edeen chas*

forbidden забранен *zabranen*

forecast прогноза *prognoza*

forehead чело *chelo*

foreign чужд *choosht*

foreigner чужденец *choozhdenets*

forest гора *gora*

forget забравям/да забравя *zabravyam/ da zabravya*

fork вилица *veelitsa*

form (document) формуляр *formulyar*, бланка *blanka*

former предишен *predeeshen*

forward (adv) напред *napret*

four-star petrol бензин А95 *benzeen A devedeset ee pet*

fracture счупване *schoopvaneh*

fragile чупливо *choopleevo*

free свободен *svoboden*; (without paying) безплатен *besplaten*

freezer фризер *freezer*

Friday петък *petuk*

fridge хладилник *Hladeelnik*

fried пържен *purzhen*

friend приятел *pri-yatel* (m), приятелка (f) *pri-yatelka*

from от *ot*; **from ... to ...** от ... до ... *ot ...do ...*

front предна част *predna chast*; **in front of** пред *pret*

fry пържа/да изпържа *purzha/da ispurzha*

frying pan тиган *tigan*

full пълен *pulen*; **full of** пълен с *pulen s*; **everything is full** всичко е заето *fseechko eh za-eto*

full board пълен пансион *pulen pansi-on*

full fare, full price без намаление *bez namaleni-eh* **71**

funfair луна парк *loona park*

furnished мебелиран *mebeleeran*

fuse бушон *booshon*

G

gallery галерия *galeri-ya*

game игра *igra* **79**

garage гараж *garash* **33**

garden градина *gradeena*

gas газ *gas*

gas cylinder газова бутилка *gazova booteelka*

gastric flu стомашен грип *stomashen greep*

gate изход *eesHot*

gauze мрежа *mrezha*

gay гей *gey*

gearbox скоростна кутия *skorostna kootee-ya*

general общ *opsht*

gents' (toilet) мъже *muzheh*

get получавам/да получа *poloochavam/ da poloocha*; **to get home** връщам се/да се върна вкъщи *vrushtam seh/da seh vurna fkushti*

get back връщам се/да се върна *vrushtam seh/da seh vurna*

get by оправям се/да се оправя *opravyam seh/da seh opravya*

get off махам/да махна *maHam/da maHna*

get up ставам/да стана *stavam/da stana*

gift подарък *podaruk*

gift-wrap (v) опаковам като подарък *opakovam kato podaruk*

girl момиче *momecheh*

girlfriend приятелка *pri-yatelka*

give давам/да дам *davam/da dam*

give back връщам/да върна *vrushtam/da vurna*

glass чаша *chasha*; **a glass of water/of wine** чаша вода/вино *chasha voda/veeno*

glasses очила *ochila*

gluten-free безглутенов *bezglootenof*

go отивам/да отида *oteevam/da oteeda*; **to go to Sofia/to Bulgaria** отивам в София/България *oteevam fsofi-ya/vbulgari-ya*; **we're going home tomorrow** заминаваме си утре *zaminavameh see ootreh*

go away заминавам/да замина *zaminavam/da zameena*

go down слизам/да сляза *sleezam/da slyaza*

go in влизам/да вляза *vleezam/da vlyaza*

go out излизам/да изляза *izleezam/da izlyaza*

go up изкачвам се/да се изкача *iskachvam seh/da seh iskachuh*

golf голф *golf*

golf course игрище за голф *igreeshteh za golf*

good добър *dobur*; **good morning** добро утро *dobro ootro*; **good afternoon** добър ден *dobur den*; **good evening** добър вечер *dobur vecher*

goodbye довиждане *doveezhdaneh*

goodnight лека нощ *leka nosht*

goods стоки *stoki*
GP семеен лекар *seme-en lekar*
grams грама *grama*
grass трева *treva*
great страхотен *straHoten*
Great Britain Великобритания *veleekobritaniya*
green зелен *zelen*
grey сив *seef*
grocer's плод и зеленчук *plot ee zelenchook*
ground земя *zemya*; **on the ground** на земята *na zemyata*
ground floor партер *parter*
ground sheet платно *platno*, платнище *platneeshta*
group група *groopa*
grow раста/да порасна *rastuh/da porastna*
guarantee гаранция *garantsi-ya*
guest гост *gost* (m), гостенка *gostenka* (f)
guest house пансион *pansi-on*
guide екскурзовод *ekskoorzovot*; програма *programa* 64
guidebook пътеводител *putevodeetel*
guided tour обиколка с екскурзовод *obikolka sekskoorzovot*
gynaecologist гинеколог *ginekolok*

hair коса *kosa*
hairdresser фризьор *frizyor*
hairdrier сешоар *sesho-ar*
half половин *poloveen*; **half a litre/kilo** половин литър/кило *poloveen leetur/kilo*; **half an hour** половин час *poloveen chas* **an hour and a half** час и половина *chas ee poloveena*
half-board полупансион *poloopansi-on*
hand ръка *ruka*
handbag ръчна чанта *ruchna chanta*
handbrake ръчна спирачка *ruchna spirachka*
handicapped: handicapped person инвалид *invaleet*
handkerchief носна кърпа *nosna kurpa*
hand luggage ръчен багаж *ruchen bagash* 28
hand-made ръчен *ruchen*

hangover махмурлук *maHmoorlook*
happen случва се *sloochva seh*
happy щастлив *shtastleef*
hard твърд *tvurt*, (difficult) труден *trooden*
hardly: hardly any почти никак *pochtee neekak*
hat шапка *shapka*
hate мразя *mrazya*
have имам *eemam*; **not have** нямам *nyamam*; **to have breakfast/dinner/lunch** закусвам/вечерям/обядвам *zakoosvam/vecheryam/obyadvam*
have to трябва *tryabva*; **I have to go** трябва да отида *tryabva da oteeda*
hay fever сенна хрема *senna Hrema*
he той *toy*
head глава *glava*
headache: to have a headache боли ме главата *bolee meh glavata*
headlight фар *far*
health здраве *zdraveh*
hear чувам/да чуя *choovam/da choo-ya*
heart сърце *surtseh*
heart attack сърдечен удар *surdechen oodar*, инфаркт *infarkt*
heat горещина *goreshtina*
heating отопление *otopleni-eh*
heavy тежък *tezhuk*
hello здравей *zdravey* (sing) здравейте *zdraveyteh* (pl)
helmet каска *kaska*
help (noun) помощ *pomosht* 113; **to call for help** викам помощ *veekam pomosht*; **help!** помощ! *pomosht!*
help (v) помагам/да помогна *pomagam/ da pomogna*
her (pronoun) нея *ne-ya*; (possessive) неин *ne-in*
here тук *took*; **here is/are** ето *eto*; **here you are** заповядай (sing)/заповядайте (pl) *zapovyaday/zapovyadayteh*
hers неин *ne-in*
hi! здрасти *zdrasti*
hi-fi уредба *ooredba*
high висок *visok*
high blood pressure високо кръвно налягане *visoko kruvno nalyaganeh*
hiking ходене *Hodeneh* 75, 76; **to go hiking** ходя на планина *Hodya na planina*
hill хълм *Hulm*

him него *nego*
himself себе си *sebeh see*
hip ханш *Hansh*
hire: for hire под наем *pod na-em*
hire (v) (people) наемам/да наема *na-emam/da na-ema*; (things) вземам/да взема под наем *vzemam/da vzema pod na-em* **34, 74, 77**
his негов *negof*
hitchhike пътувам на стоп *putoovam na stop*
hitchhiking пътуване на стоп *putoovaneh na stop*
hold държа *durzhuh*
hold on! (on the phone) почакайте *pochakayteh*
holiday(s) празник *praznik*, празници *praznitsi*, почивни дни *pocheevni dni*; **on holiday** на почивка *na pocheefka*
holiday camp (Br) ваканционно селище *vakantsi-onno selishteh*, курорт *koorort*
home дом *dom*; **at home** вкъщи *fkushti*; **to go home** отивам си вкъщи *oteevam see fkushti*
homosexual хомосексуалист *Homoseksoo-aleest*
honest честен *chesten*
honeymoon меден месец *meden mesets*
horse кон *kon*
hospital болница *bolnitsa*
hostel туристическа спалня *tooristeecheska spalnya*; общежитие *opshtezheeti-eh*
hot горещ *goresht*; **it's hot** горещо е *goreshto eh*; **hot drink** топла напитка *topla napeetka*
hot chocolate топъл шоколад *topul shokolat*
hotel хотел *Hotel*
hotplate котлон *kotlon*
hour час *chas*; **an hour and a half** час и половина *chas ee poloveena*
house къща *kushta*
housework домакинска работа *domakeenska rabota*; **to do the housework** домакинствам *domakeenstvam*
how как *kak*; **how are you?** как си (sing)/сте (pl)? *kak see/kak steh?*
hunger глад *glat*

hungry: to be hungry гладен съм *gladen sum*
hurry: to be in a hurry бързам *burzam*
hurry (up) побързай *poburzay* (sing)/ побързайте *poburzayteh* (pl)
hurt: it hurts боли *bolee*; **my leg hurts** боли ме кракът *bolee meh krakuh*
husband съпруг *suprook*

I аз *as*; **I'm English** аз съм англичанин/ англичанка *as sum anglichanin/ anglichanka*; **I'm 22 (years old)** на 22 години съм *na dvayset ee dveh godeeni sum*
ice лед *let*
ice cube кубче лед *koopche let*
identity card лична карта *leechna karta*
identity papers документи за самоличност *dokoomenti za samoleechnost*
if ако *ako*
ill болен *bolen*
illness болест *bolest*
immediate незабавен *nezabaven*; **immediately** незабавно *nezabavno*
important важен *vazhen*
impossible невъзможен *nevuzmozhen*
in в/във *v/vuf*; **in England/2007/ Bulgarian** в Англия *f Angli-ya*/през 2007 *pres 2007*/на български *na bulgarski*; **in the 19th century** през деветнайсети век *pres devetnaysti vek*; **in an hour** след един час *slet edeen chas*
included включен *fklyuchen* **40, 43, 51**
including включително *fklyucheetelno*
independent независим *nezaveesim*
indicator мигач *migach*
infection инфекция *infektsi-ya*, възпаление *vuspaleni-eh*
information информация *informatsi-ya*
injection инжекция *inzhektsi-ya*
injured ранен *ranen*
inquiries справки *sprafki*
insect насекомо *nasekomo*
insecticide инсектицид *insektitseed*
inside вътре *vutreh*
insomnia безсъние *bessuni-eh*
instant coffee нескафе *neskafeh*

instead вместо *vmesto*; **instead of** вместо *vmesto*

insurance застраховка *zastraHofka*

intend to... имам намерение да ... *eemam namereni-eh da...*

international международен *mezhdoonaroden*

international money order международен паричен превод *mezhdoonaroden pareechen prevot*

Internet интернет *eenternet*

Internet café интернет кафе *eenternet kafeh* 98

interval (in play, film) антракт *antrakt*

invite каня/да поканя *kanya/da pokanya*

Ireland ирландия *Irlandi-ya*

Irish ирландски *irlantski*

iron (noun) ютия *yutee-ya*

iron (v) гладя *glad-ya*

island остров *ostrof*

it то *to*; **it's beautiful** красиво е *kraseevo eh*; **it's warm** топло е *toplo eh*

itchy: it's itchy сърби *surbee*

item вещ *vesht*; **item of luggage** брой багаж *broy bagash*

J

jacket яке *yakeh*

January януари *yanoo-ari*

jetlag: to have jetlag страдам от часовата разлика *stradam ot chasoevata razlika*

jeweller's бижутерски магазин *bizhooterski magazeen*

jewellery бижута *bizhoota*

job работа *rabota*

jogging джогинг *dzhogink*

journey пътуване *putoovaneh*

jug кана *kana*

juice сок *sok*

July юли *yuli*

jumper пуловер *poolover*

June юни *yuni*

just: just before току-що *tokoo-shto*; **just a little** само малко *samo malko*; **just one** само един *samo edeen*; **I've just arrived** току-що пристигнах *tokoo-shto pristeegnaH*; **just in case** за всеки случай *za fseki sloochay*

K

kayak кану каяк *kanoo kayak*

keep пазя/да запазя *pazya/da zapazya*; **to keep doing** продължавайте да *produlzhavayteh da*

key ключ *klyuch*; клавиш *klaveesh* 34, 40, 43

kidney бъбрек *bubrek*

kill убивам/да убия *oobeevam/da oobee-ya*

kilometre километър *kilometur*

kind: what kind of...? какъв вид...? *kakuf veet...?*

kitchen кухня *kooHnya*

knee коляно *kolyano*

knife нож *nosh*

knock down събарям/да съборя *subaryam/da suborya*

know знам *znam*; **I don't know** не знам *neh znam*

L

ladies' (toilet) жени *zhenee*

lake езеро *ezero*

lamp лампа *lampa*

landmark забележителност *zabelezheetelnost*

landscape пейзаж *peyzash*

language език *ezeek*

laptop лаптоп *laptop*

last (adj) последен *posleden*; **last night** снощи *snoshti*; **last year** миналата година *meenalata godeena*

last: it lasts трае *tra-eh*; **does it last?** трайно ли е? *trayno lee eh?*

late: it's late късно е *kusno eh*; **to be late** закъснявам/да закъснея *zakusnyavam/da zakusne-ya*

later по-късно *po-kusno*

laugh смея се *sme-ya seh*

lawyer адвокат *advokat*

leaflet листовка *listofka*

leak: it's leaking тече *techeh*

learn уча/да науча *oocha/da na-oocha*

least: the least най-малък *nay-maluk*; **at least** поне *poneh*

leave тръгвам/да тръгна *trugvam/da trugna*; заминавам/да замина

zaminavam/da zameena
left останал ostanal **there are two tickets left** останали са два билета ostanali sa dva bileta; **we have four days left** остават ни четири дни ostavat nee chetiri dnee
left ляв lyaf; **to the left (of)** наляво/вляво от nalyavo/vlyavo ot
left-luggage (office) гардероб garderop
leg крак krak
lend давам/да дам назаем davam/da dam naza-em
lens обектив obekteef
lenses лещи leshti
less по-малко po-malko; **less than** по-малко от po-malko ot
lesson урок oorok
let: let's хайде да Haydeh da
letter писмо pismo
letterbox пощенска кутия poshtenska kootee-ya
library библиотека bibli-oteka
life живот zhivot
lift асансьор asansyor 40
light (adj) лек lek; **light blue** светло син svetlo seen
light (noun) светлина svetlina; **do you have a light?** имате ли запалка? eemateh lee zapalka?
light (v) паля/да запаля palya/da zapalya
light bulb крушка krooshka
lighter запалка zapalka
lighthouse фар far
like (adv) като kato
like (v) харесвам/да харесам Haresfam/da Haresam 21, 22; **I'd like...** искам/бих искал eeskam/beeH eeskal; **would you like...?** желаете ли… zhela-eteh lee…?
line линия leeni-ya 31
lip устна oostna
listen слушам sloosham
listings magazine (културна) програма (kooltoorna) programa
litre литър leetur
little (adj) малък maluk
little (adv) малко malko
live живея zhive-ya
live: live music музика на живо moozika na zheevo
liver черен дроб cheren drop

living room всекидневна fsekidnevna, хол Hol
local местен mesten; **local time** местно време mestno vremeh; **local call** градски разговор gratski razgovor
lock (noun) брава brava
lock (v) заключвам/да заключа zaklyuchvam/da zaklyucha
long дълъг duluk; **a long time** дълго dulgo; **a long time ago** отдавна otdavna; **how long… ?** колко време …? kolko vremeh …?
look виждам/да видя veezhdam/da veedya 85; **to look tired** изглеждам уморен izglezhdam oomoren
look after грижа се за greezha seh za
look at гледам gledam
look for търся tursya
lorry камион kami-on
lose губя/да загубя goobya/da zagoobya; **to get lost** да се загубя da seh zagoobya; **to be lost** загубих се zagoobiH seh 15
lot: a lot (of) много mnogo
loud силен seelen
love обичам obeecham; **I'd love to** с удоволствие soodovolstvi-eh
lovely прекрасен prekrasen
low нисък neesuk
low blood pressure ниско кръвно налягане neesko kruvno nalyaganeh
low-fat обезмаслен obezmaslen
luck късмет kusmet
lucky: to be lucky имам късмет eemam kusmet
luggage багаж bagash 28
lukewarm хладък Hladuk
lunch обяд obyat; **to have lunch** обядвам obyadvam
lung бял дроб byal drop
luxury (noun) лукс looks
luxury (adj) луксозен looksozen

M

madam (term of address) госпожо! gospozho!
magazine списание spisani-eh
maiden name моминско име momeensko eemeh

mail поща *poshta*

main главен *glaven*

main course основно ястие *osnovno yasti-eh*

make правя *pravya*

man мъж *mush*

manage успявам/да успея *oospyavam/da oospe-ya*; **to manage to do something** да успея да направя нещо *da oospe-ya da napravya neshto*

manager управител *oopravitel*

many много *mnogo*; **how many?** колко? *kolko?*; **how many times…?** колко пъти …? *kolko puti…?*

map карта *karta* **15, 31, 69**

March март *mart*

marina яхтено пристанище *yaHteno pristanishteh*

market пазар *pazar* **83**

married женен *zhenen* (m) омъжена *omuzhena* (f)

Mass служба *sloozhba*

match (for fire) кибрит *kibreet*; (game) мач *mach*

material плат *plat*, материал *materi-al*

matter: it doesn't matter няма значение *nyama znacheni-eh*

mattress дюшек *dyushek*

May май *my*

maybe може би *mozheh bee*

me мене *meneh*; **me too** и аз *ee as*

meal ядене *yadeneh*

mean искам да кажа *eeskam da kazha*; **what does … mean?** какво значи …? *kakvo znachi…?*

medicine лекарство *lekarstvo*

medium среден *sreden*; (meat) не препечено *nе prepecheno*

meet срещам (се)/да (се) срещна *sreshtam (seh)/da (seh) sreshtna* **63**

meeting среща *sreshta*; **to have a meeting with** да се срещна с *da seh sreshna s*

member член *chlen*

menu меню *menyu*

message съобщение *su-opshteni-eh* **102**

meter измервателен уред *izmervatelen oored*

metre метър *metur*

microwave микровълнова печка *meekrovulnova pechka*

midday обед *obet*

middle среда *sreda*; **in the middle (of)** в средата на *fsredata na*

midnight полунощ *poloonosht*

might: it might rain може да вали *mozheh da valee*

mill воденица *vodeneetsa*

mind: I don't mind нямам нищо против *nyamam neeshto proteef*

mine мой *moy*

mineral water минерална вода *mineralna voda*

minister министър *mineestur*

minute минута *minoota*; **at the last minute** в последната минута *fposlednata minoota*

mirror огледало *ogledalo*

Miss госпожица *gospozhitsa*; (term of address) госпожице! *gospozhitseh!*

miss изпускам/да изпосна *ispooskam/da ispoosna* **28, 31**; **we missed the train** изпуснахме влака *ispoosnaHmeh vlaka*; **there are two… missing** липсват два/две… *leepsvat dva/dveh…*; **I'll miss you** ще ми липсваш *shteh mee leepsvash*

mistake грешка *greshka*; **to make a mistake** правя грешка *pravya greshka*

mobile (phone) мобилен телефон *mobeelen telefon* **102**

modern модерен *moderen*

moisturizer овлажнител *ovlazhneetel*, (cream) хидратант *Hidratant*

moment момент *moment*; **at the moment** в момента *fmomenta*

monastery манастир *manasteer*

Monday понеделник *ponedelnik*

money пари *paree*

month месец *mesets*

monument паметник *pametnik*

mood: to be in a good/bad mood в добро/в лошо настроение съм *vdobro/flosho nastro-eni-eh sum*

moon луна *loona*

moped мотопед *motopet*

more повече *povecheh*, още *oshteh*; **more than** повече от *povecheh ot*; **much more, a lot more** много повече *mnogo povecheh*; **there's no more…** няма повече… *nyama povecheh…*

morning сутрин *sootrin*

morning-after pill таблетка против

забременяване *tabletka proteef zabremenyavaneh* **110**
mosque джамия *dzhamee-ya*
mosquito комар *komar*
most: the most най-големият *nay-golemi-yat*; **most people** повечето хора *povecheto Hora*
mother майка *mayka*
motorbike мотор *motor*
motorway магистрала *magistrala*
mountain планина *planina*
mountain bike планинско колело *planeensko kolelo*, байк *bayk*
mountain hut хижа *Heeza*
mouse мишка *meeshka*
mouth уста *oosta*
move: to move to премествам се/да се преместя *premestvam seh/da seh premestya*
movie филм *feelm*
Mr господин *gospodeen*
Mrs госпожа *gospozha*
much: how much? много *mnogo*; **how much is it?**, **how much does it cost?** колко струва *kolko stroova?*
muscle мускул *mooskool*
museum музей *moozey*
music музика *moozika*
must трябва *tryabva*; **it must be 5 o'clock** сигурно е пет часа *seegoorno eh pet chasuh*; **I must go** трябва да тръгвам *tryabva da trugvam*
my моят *mo-yat*
myself себе си *sebeh see*

N

nail нокът *nokut*
naked гол *gol*
name име *eemeh*; **my name is...** казвам се ... *kazvam seh...*
nap почивка *pocheefka*; **to have a nap** да си поспя *da see pospya*
napkin салфетка *salfetka*
nappy пелена *pelena*
national holiday национален празник *natsi-onalen praznik*
nature природа *priroda*
near близо *bleezo*; **near the beach** близо до плажа *bleezo do plazha*; **the**

nearest ... най-близкият... *nay-bleeski-yat...*
necessary необходим *ne-opHodeem*
neck врат *vrat*
need имам нужда от *eemam noozhda ot*
neighbour съсед *suset*
neither: neither do I и аз не *ee as neh*; **neither... nor...** нито... нито ... *neeto... neeto...*
nervous притеснен *pritesnen*
never никога *neekoga*
new нов *nof*
news новини *novinee*
newsagent продавач на вестници *prodavach na vesnitsi*
newspaper вестник *vesnik*
newsstand павилион *pavili-on*
next следващ *sledvasht*
New Year нова година *nova godeena*
nice хубав *Hoobaf*
night нощ *nosht* **39, 42**
nightclub нощен клуб *noshten kloop*
nightdress нощница *noshtnitsa*
no не *neh*; **no, thank you** не , благодаря *neh, blagodaryuh*; **no idea** нямам представа *nyamam pretstava*; **no smoking** пушенето забранено *poosheneto zabraneno*
nobody никой *neekoy*
noise шум *shoom*; **to make a noise** вдигам/да вдигна шум *vdeegam/da vdeegna shoom*
noisy шумно *shoomno*
non-drinking water непитейна вода *nepiteyna voda*
none никакъв *neekakuf*
non-smoker непушач *nepooshach*
noon обед *obet*
north север *sever*; **in the north** на север *na sever*; **(to the) north of** на север от *na sever ot*
nose нос *nos*
not не *neh*; **not yet** още не *oshteh neh*; **not any** никакъв *neekakuf*; **not at all** никакъв *neekakuf*
note бележка *beleshka*
notebook бележник *belezhnik*
nothing нищо *neeshto*
November ноември *no-emvri*
now сега *sega*
nowadays сега *sega*

nowhere никъде *neekudeh*
number брой *broy*; номер *nomer*
nurse сестра *sestra*

obvious очевиден *ocheveeden*
occasionally понякога *ponyakoga*
o'clock: one o'clock един часа *edeen chasa*; **three o'clock** три часа *tree chasa*
October октомври *oktomvri*
occupation професия *profesi-ya*
occupied зает *za-et*
of на *na*
offer предлагам/да предложа *predlagam/da predlozha*
office офис *ofis*; **ticket office** билетен център *bileten tsentur*
often често *chesto*
oil масло *maslo*
ointment унгвент *oongvent*
OK окей *okey*, добре *dobreh*
old стар *star*; **how old are you?** на колко години сте? *na kolko godeeni steh?*; **old people** стари хора *stari Hora*
on на *na*; **it's on at...** дават го на ...*davat go na...*
once някога *nyakoga*; веднъж *vednush*; **once a day** веднъж на ден *vednush na den*; **once an hour** на всеки час *na fseki chas*
one един *edeen* една *edna* едно *edno*
only само *samo*
open *(adj)* отворен *otvoren*
open *(v)* отварям/да отворя *otvaryam/da otvorya*
open-air на открито *na otkreeto*
operate опeрирам *opereeram*
operation: to have an operation правят ми операция *pravyat mee operatsiya*
opinion мнение *mneni-eh*; **in my opinion** според мен *sporet men*
opportunity възможност *vuzmozhnost*
opposite *(adj)* обратен *obraten*
opposite *(prep)* срещу *sreshtoo*
optician's оптика *optika*
or или *ilee*
orange портокал *portokal*

orchestra оркестър *orkestur*
order *(noun)* поръчка *poruchka*; ред *ret*; **out of order** не работи *neh raboti*
order *(v)* поръчвам/да поръчам *poruchvam/da porucham* **48, 49**
organic органичен *ogranichen*
organize организирам *organizeeram*
other друг *drook*; **others** други *droogi*
otherwise иначе *eenacheh*
our наш *nash*
ours наш *nash*
outside вън *vun*; навън *navun*
outward journey пътуване до *putoovaneh do*
oven фурна *foorna*
over: over there там *tam*
overdone препечено *prepecheno*, изгоряло *izgoryalo*
overweight: my luggage is overweight багажът ми е над лимита *bagazhut mee eh nat limeeta*
owe дължа *dulzhuh* **51**
own *(adj)* собствен *sopstven*; **my own** свой *svoy*
own *(v)* притежавам *pritezhavam*
owner собственик *sopstvenik* (m), собственичка *sopstvenichka* (f)

pack: to pack one's suitcase приготвям си куфара *prigotvyam see koofara*
package holiday пакетна почивка *paketna pocheefka*
packed опакован *opakovan*
packet пакет *paket*
painting картина *karteena*
pair чифт *cheeft*; двойка *dvoyka*; **a pair of socks** чифт чорапи *cheeft chorapi*; **a pair of shorts** шорти *shorti*
palace дворец *dvorets*
pants гащи *gashti*
paper хартия *Harteeya*; **paper napkin** хартиена салфетка *Hartee-ena salfetka*; **paper tissue** хартиена кърпичка *Hartee-ena kurpichka*
parcel колет *kolet*
pardon? моля? *molya?*
parents родители *rodeeteli*

park (noun) парк *park*
park (v) паркирам *parkeeram*
parking space паркинг *parkink*
part част *chast*; **to be a part of**
участвам *oochastvam*
partner приятел *pri-yatel*
party събиране *subeeraneh*, парти *parti*,
купон *koopon*
pass (noun) карта *karta*, пропуск *propoosk*
pass (v) минавам/да мина *minavam/da*
meena
passenger пътник *putnik*
passport паспорт *pasport*
past (noun) минало *meenalo*
past (prep) (with time) след *slet*:**past**
the bank покрай *pokray*; **a quarter**
past ten десет и петнайсет *deset ee*
petnayset
path пътека *puteka* 76
patient пациент *patsi-ent* (m),
пациентка (f) *patsi-entka*
pay плащам/да платя *plashtam/da*
platyuh 82, 83
pedestrian пешеходец *pesheHodets*
pedestrianized street пешеходна зона
pesheHodna zona
pee пишкам *peeshkam*
peel беля/да обеля *belya/da obelya*;
I peel беля се/да се обеля *belya seh/da*
seh obelya
pen писалка *pisalka*
pencil молив *molif*
people хора *Hora*; **for how many**
people? за колко души? *za kolko dooshi?*
per на *na*; **per person** на човек *na chovek*
percent процент *protsent*
perfect съвършен *suvurshen*, перфектен
perfekten
perfume парфюм *parfyum*
perhaps може би *mozheh bee*
periods менструация *menstroo-atsi-ya*
person човек *chovek*
personal stereo уокман *oo-okman*
petrol бензин *benzeen*
petrol station бензиностанция
benzeenostantsi-ya
phone (noun) телефон *telefon*
phone (v) обаждам се/да се обадя
obazhdam seh/da seh obadya 101
phone box телефонна кабина *telefonna*
kabeena

phone call обаждане по телефона
obazhdane po telefona; **to make a phone**
call обаждам се/да се обадя *obazhdam*
seh /da seh obadya
phonecard фонокарта *fonokarta* 101
phone number телефонен номер
telefonen nomer
photo снимка *sneemka* 89; **to take**
a photo снимам *sneemam*; **to take**
someone's photo снимам някого
sneemam nyakogo 88
phrasebook разговорник *razgovornik*
picnic пикник *peeknik*; **to have a picnic**
да си направя пикник *da see napravya*
peeknik
pie сладкиш *slatkeesh*
piece парче *parcheh*; **a piece of** парче
parcheh; **a piece of fruit** парче плод
parcheh plot
piles хемороиди *Hemero-eedi*
pill таблетка *tabletka*; **to be on the pill**
взимам противозачатъчни *vzeemam*
protivozachatuchni
pillow възглавница *vuzglavnitsa*
pillowcase калъфка за възглавница
kalufka za vuzglavnitsa
PIN (number) пин код *pin kot*
pink розов *rozof*
pity: it's a pity жалко *zhalko*
place място *myasto*
plan план *plan*
plane самолет *samolet*
plant растение *rasteni-eh*
plaster (cast) гипс *geeps*
plastic пластмасов *plasmasof*
plastic bag найлонов плик *naylonof pleek*
plate чиния *chinee-ya*
platform перон *peron*, коловоз *kolovos*
31
play (noun) игра *igra*; (theatre) пиеса
pi-esa
play (v) играя *igra-ya*
please моля *molya*
pleased доволен *dovolen*; **pleased to**
meet you! приятно ми е *pri-yatno*
mee eh
pleasure удоволствие *oodovolstvi-eh*
plenty много *mnogo*
plug (electrical) щепсел *shtepsel*
plug in включвам в контакта *fklyuchvam*
fkontakta

plumber водопроводчик *vodoprovotchik*
point точка *tochka*
police полиция *poleetsi-ya*
policeman полицай *politsay*
police station полицейско управление *politseysko oopravleni-eh*
police woman полицайка *politsayka* **113**
poor беден *beden*
port пристанище *pristanishteh*
portrait портрет *portret*
possible възможен *vuzmozhen*
post поща *poshta*
postbox пощенска кутия *poshtenska kootee-ya* **95**
postcard пощенска картичка *poshtenska kartichka*
postcode пощенски код *poshtenski kot*
poste restante до поискване *do po-eeskvaneh*
poster плакат *plakat*
postman пощальон *poshtalyon*
post office поща *poshta* **95**
pot тенджера *tendzhera*
pound лира *leera*, паунд *pa-oont*
powder пудра *poodra*
practical практичен *prakteechen*
pram количка *koleechka*
prefer предпочитам/да предпочета *pretpocheetam/da pretpochetuh*
pregnant бременна *bremenna* **108**
prepare приготвям/да приготвя *prigotvyam/da prigotvya*
prescription рецепта *retsepta*
present подарък *podaruk*
press натискам/да натисна *nateeskam/da nateesna*
previous предишен *predeeshen*
price цена *tsena*
private частен *chasten*
prize награда *nagrada*
probably вероятно *vero-yatno*
problem проблем *problem*
proceed отправям се/да се отправя *otpravyam seh/da seh otpravya*; продължавам/да продължа *produlzhavam/da produlzhuh*
product продукт *prodookt*
profession професия *profesi-ya*
programme програма *programa*
promise обещавам/да обещая *obeshtavam/da obeshta-ya*

propose предлагам/да предложа *predlagam/da predlozha*
protect предпазвам/да предпазя *pretpazvam/da pretpazya*
proud (of) горд (с) *gort (s)*
provide: … is provided … осигурен … *osigooren*
public обществен *opshtestven*; **public transport** градски транспорт *gratski transport*
public holiday официален празник *ofitsi-alen praznik*
pull дърпам/да дръпна *durpam/da drupna*
purple лилав *lilaf*
purpose: on purpose нарочно *narochno*
purse портмоне *portmoneh*
push бутам/да бутна *bootam/da bootna*
pushchair количка *koleechka*
put слагам/да сложа *slagam/da slozha*
put out гася/да изгася *gasyuh/da izgasyuh*
put up (lodge) настанявам /да настаня *nastanyavam/da nastanyuh*
put up with примирявам се/да се примиря *primiryavam seh/da seh primiryuh*

Q

quality качество *kachestvo*; **of good/bad quality** с добро/лошо качество *s dobro/losho kachestvo*
quarter четвърт *chetvurt*; **a quarter of an hour** 15 минути *petnayset minooti*; **a quarter to ten** десет без петнайсет *deset bes petnayset*
quay кей *key*
question въпрос *vupros*
queue (noun) опашка *opashka*
queue (v) чакам на опашка *chakam na opashka*
quick бърз *burs*
quickly бързо *burzo*
quiet тих *teeH*
quite съвсем *sufsem*; **quite a lot of** доста *dosta*

R

racist расист *raseest*

racket ракета *raketa*
radiator радиатор *radi-ator*
radio радио *radi-o*
radio station радиостанция *radi-ostantsi-ya*
rain дъжд *dusht*
rain: *(v)* **it's raining** вали (дъжд) *valee (dusht)*
raincoat шлифер *shleefer*
random: at random случайно *sloochayno*
rape изнасилване *iznaseelvaneh*
rare рядък *ryaduk*; *(meat)* алангле *alangleh*
rarely рядко *ryatko*
rather твърде *tvurdeh*
raw суров *soorof*
razor бръснач *brusnach*
razor blade бръснарско ножче *brusnarsko noshcheh*
reach стигам/да стигна *steegam/da steegna*
read чета/да прочета *chetuh/da prochetuh*
ready готов *gotof*
reasonable разумен *razoomen*
receipt разписка *raspiska*, бележка *beleshka*; фактура *faktoora* **83, 109**
receive получавам/да получа *poloochavam/da poloocha*
recently напоследък *naposleduk*
reception прием *pree-em*; *(hotel)* рецепция *retsetsi-ya*; *(on phone)* връзка *vruska*; **at reception** на рецепцията *na retseptsi-yata* **42**
receptionist администратор *administrator (m)*, администраторка *administratorka (f)*
recharge зареждам/да заредя (отново) *zarezhdam/da zaredyuh (otnovo)* **101**
recipe рецепта *retsepta*
recognize познавам/да позная *poznavam/da pozna-ya*; признавам/да призная *priznavam/da prizna-ya*
recommend препоръчвам/да препоръчам *preporuchvam/da preporucham* **40, 47**
red червен *cherven*; *(hair)* риж *reesh*
red light червен светофар *cherven svetofar*
red wine червено вино *cherveno veeno*

reduce намалявам/да намаля *namalyavam/da namalyuh*
reduction намаление *namaleni-eh*
refrigerator хладилник *Hladeelnik*
refund: to get a refund получвам парите обратно *poloochavam pareeteh obratno* **86**
refund *(v)* връщам/да върна парите *vrushtam/da vurna pareeteh* **109**
refuse отказвам/да откажа *otkazvam/da otkazha*
registered регистриран *registreeran*; *(letter)* препоръчано *preporuchano*
registration number регистрационен номер *registratsi-onen nomer*
remember запомням/да запомня *zapomnyam/da zapomnya*; *(recall)* спомням си/да си спомня *spomnyam see/da see spomnya*
remind напомням/да напомня *napomnyam/da napomnya*
remove премахвам/да премахна *premaHvam/da premaHna*
rent *(noun)* наем *na-em*
rent *(v)* вземам под наем/да взема под наем *vzemam pod na-em/da vzema pod na-em* **43**; *(out)* давам под наем/да дам под наем *davam pod na-em/da dam pod na-em*
rental наем *na-em*
reopen отварям/да отворя отново *otvaryam/da otvorya otnovo*
repair ремонтирам *remonteeram*, поправям/да поправя *popravyam/da popravya* **34**; **to get something repaired** да ми поправят нещо *da mee popravyat neshto*
reply *(noun)* отговор *otgovor*
reply *(v)* отговарям/да отговоря *otgovaryam/da otgovorya*
report съобщавам/да съобщя *su-opshtavam/da su-opshtyuh*
repeat повтарям/да повторя *poftaryam/da poftorya*
reserve запазвам/да запазя *zapazvam/da zapazya* **39, 47, 48**
reserved запазен *zapazen*
rest: *(noun)* **the rest** останалите *ostanaliteh*
rest *(v)* почивам си/да си почина *pocheevam see/da see pocheena*

restaurant ресторант *restorant* 47

return *(noun)* връщане *vrushtaneh;*
  return ticket билет за отиване и
  връщане *bilet za oteevaneh ee vrushtaneh*

return *(v)* връщам (се) /да (се) върна
  vrushtam seh/da seh vurna

reverse-charge call обаждане за
  тяхна сметка *obazhdaneh za tyaHna
  smetka* 57

reverse gear задна скорост *zadna
  skorost*

review отзив *otzif,* критика *kreetika*

rheumatism ревматизъм *revmateezum*

rib ребро *rebro*

ride яздя *yazdya; (a bike)* карам *karam*

right *(noun)* право *pravo;* **to have the
  right to...** имам правото да... *eemam
  pravoto da...*

right *(adj)* десен *desen;* **to the right (of)**
  надясно (от) *nadyasno (ot)*

right: *(adv)* **right away** веднага *vednaga;*
  right beside непосредствено до
  neposretstveno do

ring *(noun)* пръстен *prusten*

ring *(v)* звъня /да звънна *zvunyuh/da
  zvunna, (call)* обаждам се/да се обадя
  obazhdam seh/da seh obadya

ripe зрял *zryal*

rip-off обир *obeer*

risk риск *reesk*

river река *reka*

road път *put; (for cars)* шосе *shoseh*

road sign пътен знак *puten znak,*
  табелка *tabelka*

rock скала *skala*

room стая *sta-ya* 39, 40

rosé wine вино розе *veeno rozeh*

round *(noun)* обиколка *obikolka, (sport)*
  рунд *roont*

round *(adj)* кръгъл *krugul*

roundabout кръгово движение *krugovo
  dvizheni-eh*

rubbish боклук *boklook;* **to take the
  rubbish out** изхвърлям/да изхвърля
  боклука *isHvurlyam/da isHvurlya boklooka*

rucksack раница *ranitsa*

rug килимче *kileemcheh, (traditional)*
  черга *cherga*

ruins развалини *razvaleenee,* останки
  ostanki; **in ruins** разрушен *razrooshen*

run out: to have run out of petrol
свърши ми бензинът *svurshi mee
benzeenut*

S

sad тъжен *tuzhen*

safe в безопасност *vbezopasnost*

safety безопасност *bezopasnost*

safety belt предпазен колан *pretpazen
  kolan*

sail плавам *plavam*

sailing платноходство *platnoHotstvo;* **to
  go sailing** да отплавам *da otplavam*

sale: for sale продава се *prodava
  seh;* **in the sale** на разпродажба *na
  rasprodazhba*

sales разпродажба *rasprodazhba*

salt сол *sol*

salted посолен *posolen*

salty солен *solen*

same същият *sushti-yat;* **the same**
  същия *sushti-yat*

sand пясък *pyasuk*

sandals сандали *sandali*

sanitary towel дамски превръзки
  damski prevruzki

Saturday събота *subota*

saucepan тиган *tigan*

save спасявам/да спася *spasyavam/da
  spasyuh; (on computer)* запазвам/да
  запазя *zapazvam/da zapazya*

say казвам *kazvam;* **how do you say... ?**
  как се казва...? *kak seh kazva...?*

scared: to be scared (of) страх ме е
  (от) *straH meh eh (ot)*

scenery пейзаж *peyzash*

school училище *oocheelishteh*

scissors ножица *nozhitsa*

scoop: one/two scoop(s) *(of ice cream)*
  една топка/две топки *edna topka/dveh
  topki*

scooter скутер *skooter*

scotch *(whisky)* скоч уиски *skoch weeski*

Scotland Шотландия *shotlandi-ya*

Scottish шотландски *shotlantski*

scuba diving подводен спорт *podvoden
  sport,* гмуркане *gmoorkaneh*

sea море *moreh*

seafood морски специалитети *morski
  spetsi-aliteti*

seasick: to be seasick гади ми се *gadi*

mee seh, имам морска болест *eemam morska bolest*
seaside: at the seaside на море *na moreh*
seaside resort морски курорт *morski koorort*
season сезон *sezon*
seat място *myasto*; **take a seat!** заповядайте! *zapovyadayteh!*, седнете! *sedneteh!*
sea view изглед към морето *eezglet kum moreto*
seaweed водорасло *vodoraslo*
second втори *ftori*
second class втора класа *ftora klasa*
secondary school основно училище *osnovno oocheelishteh*
second-hand втора ръка *ftora ruka*, на старо *na staro*
secure сигурен *seegooren*
security охрана *oHrana*
see виждам/да видя *veezhdam/da veedya*; **see you later!** довиждане *doveezhdaneh*; **see you soon!** до скоро! *do skoro!*; **see you tomorrow!** до утре *do ootreh*; **to see home** изпращам/да изпратя *isprashtam/da ispratya*
seem изглеждам *izglezhdam*; **it seems that…** изглежда, че *izglezhda, cheh*
seldom рядко *ryatko*
select избирам/да избера *izbeeram/da izberuh*
self-confidence самоувереност *samo-ooverenost*
sell продавам/да продам *prodavam/da prodam*; **sold out** продаден *prodaden*
Sellotape® тиксо *teekso*, скоч лепенка *skoch lepenka*
send пращам/да пратя *prashtam/da pratya*
sender подател *podatel*
sense (of) чувство (за) *choostvo (za)*; **it makes sense** разумно е *razoomno eh*
sensitive чувствителен *choostveetelen*
sentence изречение *izrecheni-eh*
separate отделен *otdelen*
separately отделно *otdelno*
September септември *septemvri*
serious сериозен *seri-ozen*
serve сервирам *serveeram*
service услуга *ooslooga*; обслужване *opsloozhvaneh*, сервиз *servees* 51

several няколко *nyakolko*
sex пол *pol*, секс *seks*
shade сянка *syanka*; **in the shade** на сянка *na syanka*
shame срам *sram*
shampoo шампоан *shampo-an*
shape форма *forma*
share ползвам общо *polzvam opshto*; **shared** общ *opsht*
shave бръсна се/да се обръсна *brusna seh/da seh obrusna*
shaver самобръсначка *samobrusnachka*
shaving cream крем за бръснене *krem za brusneneh*
shaving foam пяна за бръснене *pyana za brusneneh*
she тя *tya*
sheet чаршаф *charshaf*; *(of paper)* лист *leest*
shellfish мида *meeda*
shirt риза *reeza*
shock шок *shok*
shocking шокиращ *shokeerasht*
shoes обувки *oboofki*
shop магазин *magazeen*
shop assistant продавачка *prodavachka* (f) продавач *prodavach(m)*
shopkeeper собственик на магазин *sopstvenik na magazeen*
shopping пазаруване *pazaroovaneh*; **to do some/the shopping** пазарувам/да напазарувам *pazaroovam/da napazaroovam*
shopping centre търговски център *turgofski tsentur*
short къс *kus*; **I'm two… short** липсват ми две… *leepsfat mee dveh…*
short cut пряк път *pryak put*
shorts шорти *shorti*
short-sleeved с къси ръкави *skusi rukavi*
shoulder рамо *ramo*
show *(noun)* шоу *sho-oo*, представление *pretstavleni-eh*
show *(v)* показвам/да покажа *pokazvam/da pokazha*
shower душ *doosh*; **to take a shower** вземам душ *vzemam doosh*
shower gel душгел *dooshgel*
shut затварям *zatvaryam*
shy срамежлив *sramezhleef*
sick: to feel sick гади ми се *gadi mee seh*

side страна *strana*

sign *(noun)* знак *znak*

sign *(v)* подписвам/да подпиша *potpeesfam/da potpeesha*

signal сигнал *signal*

silent тих *teeH*, мълчалив *mulchaleef*

silver сребро *srebro*

silver-plated посребрен *posrebren*

since от *ot*, откакто *otkakto*

sing пея/да изпея *pe-ya/da ispe-ya*

singer певец *pevets* (m), певица *peveetsa* (f)

single единичен *edineechen*; (not married) неженен *nezhenen*

single (ticket) за отиване *za oteevaneh*

sink потъвам/да потъна *potuvam/da potuna*

sir господине *gospodeeneh*

sister сестра *sestra*

sit down сядам/да седна *syadam/da sedna*

size размер *razmer*

ski ски *skee*

ski boots обувки за ски *oboofki za skee*

skiing каране на ски *karaneh na skee*; **to go skiing** отивам да карам ски *oteevam da karam skee*

ski lift ски лифт *skee leeft*

ski pole щека *shteka*

ski resort зимен курорт *zeemen koorort*

skin кожа *kozha*

skirt пола *pola*

sky небе *nebeh*

sleep *(noun)* сън *sun*

sleep *(v)* спя *spyuh*; **to sleep with** спя с *spyuh s*

sleeping bag спален чувал *spalen chooval*

sleeping pill приспивателно *prispivatelno*

sleepy: to be sleepy спи ми се *spee mee seh*

sleeve ръкав *rukaf*

slice филия *filee-ya*

sliced нарязан *naryazan*

slide *(noun)* диапозитив *di-apositeef*

slide *(v)* пързалям се *purzalyam seh*

slow бавен *baven*

slowly бавно *bavno*

small малък *maluk*

smell *(noun)* миризма *mirizma*

smell *(v)* мириша *mireesha*; **it smells**

good/bad мирише хубаво/лошо *mireesheh Hoobavo/losho*

smile *(noun)* усмивка *oosmeefka*

smile *(v)* усмихвам се *oosmeeHvam seh*

smoke пуша *poosha*

smoker пушач *pooshach*

snack закуска *zakooska*

snow *(noun)* сняг *snyak*

snow *(v)* вали сняг *valee snyak*

so така *taka*; **so that** така, че *taka, cheh*

soap сапун *sapoon*

soccer футбол *footbol*

socks чорапи *chorapi*

some някакъв *nyakakuf*; **some people** няколко души *nyakolko dooshi*

somebody някой *nyakoy*

someone някой *nyakoy*

something нещо *neshto*; **something else** нещо друго *neshto droogo*

sometimes понякога *ponyakoga*

somewhere някъде *nyakudeh*; **somewhere else** някъде другаде *nyakudeh droogadeh*

son син *seen*

song песен *pesen*

soon скоро *skoro*

sore: to have a sore throat боли ме гърло *bolee meh gurlo*

sorry: to be sorry съжалявам *suzhalyavam*; **sorry!** извинявайте *izvinyavayteh*, прощавайте *proshtavayteh*

sort вид *veet*

south юг *yuk*; **in the south** на юг *na yuk*; **(to the) south of** на юг от *na yuk ot*

souvenir сувенир *sooveneer*

space място *myasto*

spare резервен *rezerven*

spare part резервна част *rezervna chast*

spare tyre резервна гума *rezervna gooma*

spare wheel резервно колело *rezervno kolelo*

spark plug свещ *sfesht*

sparkling water газирана вода *gazeerana voda*

speak говоря *govorya* 11, 13, 102, 103, 113; **speak up** говорете по-високо *govereteh po-visoko*

special специален *spetsi-alen*; **today's special** специалитет за деня *spetsi-alitet na denyuh* 49

speciality специалитет *spetsi-alitet*
speed скорост *skorost*; **at full speed** с пълна скорост *spulna skorost*
spell пиша/да напиша *peesha/da napeesha*; **how do you spell it?** как се пише? *kak seh peesheh?*
spend *(money)* харча/да похарча *Harcha/da poHarcha*; *(time)* прекарвам/ да прекарам *prekarvam/da prekaram*, изкарвам/да изкарам *iskarvam/da iskaram*
spice подправка *potprafka*
spicy пикантен *pikanten*
spider паяк *payak*
splinter треска *treska*
split up разделям/да разделя *razdelyam/da razdelyuh*
spoil развалям/да разваля *razvalyam/da razvalyuh*
sponge гъба *guba*
spoon лъжица *luzheetsa*
sport спорт *sport*
sports ground игрище *igreeshteh*
sporty спортен *sporten*
spot *(on face)* пъпка *pupka*; *(place)* място *myasto*
sprain: to sprain one's ankle изкълчвам/да изкълча глезена си *iskulchvam/da iskulcha glezena see*
spring пролет *prolet*
square площад *ploshtat*
stadium стадион *stadi-on*
stain петно *petno*
stained-glass windows прозорци със стъклопис *prozortsi sus stuklopees*
stairs стълби *stulbi*
stamp марка *marka* **95**
start започвам/да започна *zapochvam/ da zapochna*
starter предястие *predyasti-eh*, ордьовър *ordyovur*
state държава *durzhava*; *(condition)* състояние *sustoyani-eh*
statement декларация *deklaratsi-ya*
station гара *gara*; станция *stantsi-ya*
stay *(noun)* престой *prestoy*
stay *(v)* оставам/да остана *ostavam/da ostana*; **in a hotel** отсядам/да отседна *otsyadam/da otsedna*; **to stay in touch** обаждам се *obazhdam seh*
steal крада/да открадна *kraduh/da otkradna*

step стъпка *stupka*
sticking plaster лепенка *lepenka*
still *(все)* още *(fseh) oshteh*
still water обикновена/негазирана вода *obeeknovena/negazeerana voda*
sting *(noun)* ужилване *oozheelvaneh*
sting *(v)* ужилвам/да ужиля *oozheelvam/ da oozheelya*; **to get stung (by)** ужилен съм *oozheelen sum (m)* ужилена съм *(f) oozheelena sum*
stock: out of stock изчерпан *ischerpan*
stomach стомах *stomaH*
stone камък *kamuk*
stop *(noun)* спирка *speerka* **31**
stop *(v)* спирам/да спра *speeram/da spruh*
storey етаж *etash*
storm буря *boorya*
straight ahead, **straight on** направо *napravo*
straightaway веднага *vednaga*
strange странен *stranen*
street улица *oolitsa*
strong силен *seelen*
student студент *stoodent (m)*, студентка *stoodentka (f)* **26**
studies следване *sledvaneh*
study уча *oocha*; **to study biology** следвам биология *sledvam bi-ologi-ya*
style стил *steel*, модел *model*
subtitled със субтитри *sus sooptitri*
suburb предградие *predgradi-eh*
suffer страдам *stradam*
suggest предлагам/да предложа *predlagam/da predlozha*
suitable подходящ *potHodyasht*
suit: does it suit me? това отива ли ми? *tova oteeva lee mee?*
suitcase куфар *koofar* **28**
summer лято *lyato*
summit връх *vruH*
sun слънце *sluntseh*; **in the sun** на слънце *na sluntseh*
sunbathe пека се на слънце *pekuh seh na sluntseh*
sunburnt: to get sunburnt да изгоря *da eezgoryuh*
sun cream слънцезащитен крем *sluntsezashteeten krem*
Sunday неделя *nedelya*
sunglasses слънчеви очила *slunchevi ochila*

sunhat плажна шапка *plazhna shapka*
sunrise изгрев *izgref*
sunset залез *zales*
sunstroke слънчев удар *slunchef oodar*;
to get sunstroke получавам слънчев удар *poloochavam slunchef oodar*
supermarket супермаркет *soopermarket*
supplement добавка *dobafka*
sure сигурен *seegooren*
surf (v) карам сърф *karam surf*
surfboard сърф *surf*
surfing каране на сърф *karaneh na surf*;
to go surfing отивам да карам сърф *oteevam da karam surf*
surgery лекарски кабинет *lekarski kabinet*
surgical spirit медицински спирт *meditseenski speert*
surname фамилно име *fameelno eemeh*
surprise (noun) изненада *iznenada*
surprise (v) изненадвам/да изненадам *iznenadvam/da iznenadam*
swallow гълтам/да глътна *gultam/da glutna*
sweat пот *pot*
sweater блуза *blooza*
sweet (noun) бонбон *bonbon*
sweet (adj) сладък *sladuk*
swim: (noun) **to go for a swim** отивам да поплувам *oteevam da poploovam*
swim (v) плувам *ploovam*
swimming плуване *ploovaneh*
swimming pool басейн *baseyn*
swimming trunks бански *banski*
swimsuit бански костюм *banski kostyum*
switch off изключвам/да изключа *isklyuchvam/da isklyucha*
switch on включвам/да включа *fklyuchvam/da fklyucha*
switchboard operator телефонистка *telefoneestka*
swollen подут *podoot*
synagogue синагога *sinagoga*
syrup сироп *sirop*

T

table маса *masa* **47, 48**
tablespoon супена лъжица *soopena luzheetsa*

tablet таблетка *tabletka*
take вземам *vzemam*; **it takes two hours** отнема два часа *otnema dva chasa*
take off (plane) излитам/да излетя *izleetam/da izletyuh*
takeaway храна за вкъщи *Hrana za fkushti*
talk говоря *govorya*
tall висок *visok*
tampon тампон *tampon*
tan тен *ten*
tank резервоар *rezervo-ar*
tanned почернял *pochernyal*, с тен *sten*
tap кран *kran*
taste (noun) вкус *fkoos*
taste (v) опитвам/да опитам *opeetvam/da opeetam*; **it tastes of** има вкус на *eema fkoos na*
tax такса *taksa*, данък *danuk*
tax-free без мито *bez meeto*
taxi такси *taksee* **35**
taxi driver шофьор на такси *shofyor na taksee*
T-bar ски влек *skee vlek*
team отбор *otbor*
tea чай *chay*
teaspoon чаена лъжичка *cha-ena luzheechka*
teenager тийнейджър *teeneydzhur* (m) тийнейджърка *teeneydzhurka* (f)
telephone (noun) телефон *telefon*
telephone (v) обаждам се по телефона *obazhdam seh po telefona*
television телевизия *televeezi-ya*
tell казвам/да кажа *kazvam/da kazha*
temperature температура *temperatoora*; **to take one's temperature** меря си температурата *merya see temperatoorata*
temple храм *Hram*
temporary временен *vremenen*
tenant наемател *na-ematel* (m), наематепка *na-ematelka* (f)
tennis тенис *tenis*
tennis court тенискорт *teniskort*
tennis shoe маратонка *maratonka*
tent палатка *palatka*
tent peg колче *kopcheh*
terminal терминал *terminal*
terrace тераса *terasa*
terrible ужасен *oozhasen*

text message есемес *esemes*

thank благодаря *blagodaryuh*; **thank you** благодаря ти/ви *blagodaryuh tee/vee*; **thank you very much** много ти/ви благодаря *mnogo tee/vee blagodaryuh*

thanks благодарности *blagodarnosti*; **thanks to** благодарение на *blagodareni-eh na*

that онзи *onzi*; **that one** този *tozi*

that: I think that... мисля че... *meeslya cheh...*

the -ът/а (m), -та (f), -то (n), -те (pl)

theatre театър *te-atur*

theft кражба *krazhba*

their техният *teHni-yat*

theirs техен *teHen*

them на тях *na tyaH*

theme park увеселителен парк *ooveseleetelen park* луна парк *loona park*

then тогава *togava*

there там *tam*; **there is** има *eema*; **there are** има *eema*

therefore затова *zatova*

thermometer термометър *termometur*

Thermos® flask термос *termos*

these тези *tezi*; **these ones** тези *tezi*

they те *teh*; **they say that...** казват, че *kazvat, cheh*

thief крадец *kradets*

thigh бедро *bedro*

thin тънък *tunuk*

thing нещо *neshto*, предмет *predmet*; **things** неща *neshta*, предмети *predmeti*

think мисля *meeslya*

think about мисля за *meeslya za*

thirst жажда *zhazhda*

thirsty жаден *zhaden*

this този *tozi*; **this one** този *tozi*; **this evening** довечера *dovechera*; **this is** това е *tova eh*

those онези *onezi*; **those ones** онези *onezi*

throat гърло *gurlo*

throw хвърлям/да хвърля *Hvurlyam/da Hvurlya*

throw out изхвърлям/да изхвърля *isHvurlyam/da isHvurlya*

Thursday четвъртък *chetvurtuk*

ticket билет *bilet* **26, 64, 65, 70**

ticket office каса *kasa*, билетен център *bileten tsentur*

tidy подреден *podreden*

tie връзка *vruska*

tight тесен *tesen*

tights чорапогащи *chorapogashti*

time време *vremeh*; **what time is it?** колко е часът? *kolko eh chasuh?*; **from time to time** отвреме-навреме *otvremeh navremeh*; **on time** навреме *navremeh*; **three/four times** три/четири пъти *tree/chetiri puti*

time difference разлика във времето *razlika vuf vremeto*

timetable разписание *raspisani-eh* **26**

tinfoil алуминиево фолио *aloomeeni-evo foli-o*

tip бакшиш *baksheesh*

tired уморен *oomoren*

toast тост *tost*; (bread) препечени филии *prepecheni filee-i*

tobacco тютюн *tyutyun*

tobacconist's магазин за цигари *magazeen za tsigari*

today днес *dnes*

together заедно *za-edno*

toilet тоалетна *to-aletna* **11, 47**

toilet bag тоалетна чантичка *to-aletna chantichka*

toilet paper тоалетна хартия *to-aletna Hartee-ya*

toiletries козметика *kozmetika*

toll пътна такса *putna taksa*

tomorrow утре *ootreh*; **tomorrow evening** утре вечер *ootreh vecher*; **tomorrow morning** утре сутринта *ootreh sootrinta*

tongue език *ezeek*

tonight довечера *dovechera*

too прекалено *prekaleno*; **too bad** много лош *mnogo losh*; **too many** прекалено много *prekaleno mnogo*; **too much** прекалено много *prekaleno mnogo*

tooth зъб *zup*

toothbrush четка за зъби *chetka za zubi*

toothpaste паста за зъби *pasta za zubi*

top връх *vruH*; **at the top** на върха *na vurHuh*

torch фенерче *fenercheh*

touch докосвам/да докосна *dokosvam/da dokosna*

tourist турист *tooreest* (m), туристка *tooreestka(f)*

tourist information centre

туристически информационен център *tooristeecheski informatsi-onen tsentur*

tourist trap капан за туристи *kapan za tooreesti*

towards към *kum*

towel хавлиена кърпа *Havlee-ena kurpa*

town град *grat*

town centre центъра на града *tsentura na graduh*

town hall община *opshtina*

toy играчка *igrachka*

traditional традиционен *traditsi-onen*

traffic трафик *trafik*, движение *dvizheni-eh*

traffic jam задръстване *zadrustvaneh*

trailer ремарке *remarkeh*; каравана *karavana*

train влак *vlak* 31; **the train to Sofia** влакът за София *vlakut za Sofiya*

train station жепе гара *zhepeh gara*

tram трамвай *tramvay*

transfer (noun) (of money) (паричен) превод *(pareechen) prevot*

transfer (v) прехвърлям/да прехвърля preHvurlyam/da preHvurl-ya 92

translate превеждам/да преведа *prevezhdam/da prevedu*

travel agency туристическа агенция *tooristeecheska agentsi-ya*

travel пътувам *putoovam*

traveller's cheque пътнически чек *putnicheski chek*, травълър чек *travulur chek*

treat: my treat аз черпя *as cherpya*

trip екскурзия *ekskoorzi-ya*; **have a good trip!** приятен път! *pri-yaten put!*

trolley тролей *troley*

trouble: to have trouble doing something не мога да направя нещо *neh moga da napravya neshto*

trousers панталон *pantalon*

true вярно *vyarno*

try опитвам се/да се опитам *opeetvam seh/da seh opeetam*; **to try to do something** опитвам се да направя нещо *opeetvam seh da napravya neshto*

try on пробвам *probvam*

Tuesday вторник *ftornik*

tube метро *metro*

tube station станция на метрото *stantsi-ya na metroto*

turn (noun) (on road) завой *zavoy*; **it's your turn** твой ред е *tvoy ret eh (sing)*/ ваш ред е *vash ret eh (pl)*

turn (v) обръщам (се)/да (се) обърна *obrushtam seh/da seh oburna*; завивам/да завия *zaveevam/da zavee-ya*

twice два пъти *dva puti*

type (noun) тип *teep*

type (v) пиша на компютър *peesha na kompyutur*

typical типичен *tipeechen*

tyre гума *gooma*

U

umbrella чадър *chadur*

uncle вуйчо *vooycho*

uncomfortable неудобен *ne-oodoben*

under под *pot*

underground метро *metro*

underground line линия на метрото *leeni-ya na metroto*

underground station станция на метрото *stantsi-ya na metroto*

underneath под *pot*

understand разбирам/да разбера *razbeeram/da razberuh* 13

underwear бельо *belyo*

United Kingdom Обединеното кралство *obedinenoto kralstvo*

United States Съединените щати *su-edineniteh shtati*

until до(като) *do(kato)*

upset разтревожен *rastrevozhen*

upstairs на горния етаж *na gorni-ya etash*

urgent спешен *speshen*

us на нас *na nas*

use ползвам *polzvam*; използвам *ispolzvam*; **to be used for** да се използва за *da seh izpolzva za*; **I'm used to it** свикнал съм *sveeknal sum (m)*/ свикнала съм *sveeknala sum (f)*

useful полезен *polezen*

useless безполезен *bespolezen*

usually обикновено *obiknoveno*

U-turn обратен завой *obraten zavoy*

V

vacancy свободно/празно място

svobodno/prazno myasto **39**

vaccinated (against) имунизиран (срещу) *imoonizeeran (sreshtoo)*

valid (for/until) валиден (за/до) *valeeden (za/do)*; **the ticket is valid for** билетът важи за *biletut vazhee za*

valley долина *dolina*

VAT ДеДеСе *dedeseh*

vegetable зеленчук *zelenchook*

vegetarian вегетарианец *vegetari-anets* (m), вегетарианка *vegetari-anka(f)*

very много *mnogo*

view изглед *eezglet*

villa вила *veela*

village село *selo*

visa виза *veeza*

visit *(noun)* посещение *poseshteni-eh*

visit *(v)* посещавам/да посетя *poseshtavam/da posetyuh*

volleyball волейбол *voleybol*

vomit повръщам/да повърна *povrushtam/da povurna*

W

waist талия *tali-ya*

wait чакам/да изчакам *chakam/da ischakam*; **to wait for somebody** чакам някого *chakam nyakogo*; **to wait for something** очаквам нещо *ochakvam neshto*

waiter сервитьор *servityor*

waiting room чакалня *chakalnya*

waitress сервитьорка *servityorka*

wake up събуждам се/да се събудя *suboozhdam seh/da seh suboodya*

Wales Уелс *oo-els*

walk *(noun) (route)* маршрут *marshroot* **75, 76**; **to go for a walk** отивам на разходка *oteevam na rasHotka*;

walk *(v)* разхождам се/да се разходя *rasHozhdam seh/da seh rasHodya*

walking: to go walking вървя пеша *vurvya pesha*

walking boots туристически обувки *tooristeecheski oboofki*

Walkman® Уокман *oo-okman*

wallet портфейл *portfeyl*

want искам *eeskam*; **to want to do something** искам да направя нещо

eeskam da napravya neshto

warm топъл *topul*

warn предупреждавам/да предупредя *predooprezhdavam/da predoopredyuh*

wash мия/да измия *mee-ya/da izmee-ya*; **to wash one's hair** да си измия косата *da see izmee-ya kosata*

washbasin умивалник *oomivalnik*

washing: to do the washing пера/да изпера *peruh/da isperuh*

washing machine пералня *peralnya*

washing powder прах за пране *praH za praneh*

washing-up liquid препарат за миене на съдове *preparat za mee-eneh na sudoveh*

wasp оса *osa*

waste прахосвам/да прахосам *praHosvam/da praHosam*

watch *(noun)* часовник *chasovnik*

watch *(v)* наблюдавам *nablyudavam*; **watch out!** внимавай! *vnimavay!*

water вода *voda*

water heater бойлер *boyler*

waterproof водоустойчив *vodo-oostoychif*

waterskiing каране на водни ски *karaneh na vodni skee*

wave вълна *vulna*

way път *put*; **which way?** в коя посока? *fko-ya posoka?*; **in this way** по този начин *po tozi nachin*

way in вход *fHot*

way out изход *eesHot*

we ние *nee-eh*

weak слаб *slap*, отпаднал *otpadnal*

wear нося *nosya*

weather време *vremeh*; **the weather's bad** времето е лошо *vremeto eh losho*

weather forecast прогноза за времето *prognoza za vremeto* **24**

website уеб страница *wep stranitsa*

Wednesday сряда *sryada*

week седмица *sedmitsa*; **week days** работни дни *rabotni dnee*

weekend уикенд *oo-eekent*, края на седмицата *kra-ya na sedmitsata*

welcome! добре дошъл/дошла/дошли *dobreh doshul/doshla/doshlee*; **you're welcome** няма защо *nyama zashto*

well добре *dobreh*; **I'm very well** много

съм добре *mnogo sum dobreh*; **well done** *(meat)* добре опечено *dobreh opecheno*
well-known известен *izvesten*
Welsh уелски *oo-elski*
west запад *zapat*; **in the west** на запад *na zapat*; **(to the) west of** на запад от *na zapat ot*
wet мокър *mokur*
wetsuit акваланг *akvalank*
what какво *kakvo*; **what do you want?** какво искате? *kakvo eeskateh?*
wheel колело *kolelo*
wheelchair инвалидна количка *invaleedna koleechka*
when кога *koga*, когато *kogato*
where къде *kudeh*; **where is/are...?** къде е/са...? *kudeh eh/sa...?*; **where are you from?** откъде си/сте? *otkudeh see?*; **where are you going?** къде отиваш? *kudeh oteevash?*
whether дали *dalee*
which кой *koy*
while докато *dokato*
white бял *byal*;
white wine бяло вино *byalo veeno*
who кой *koy*; **who's calling?** кой се обажда? *koy seh obazhda?*
whole цял *tsyal*; **the whole cake** цялата торта *tsyalata torta*
whose чий *cheey*
why защо *zashto*
wide широк *shirok*
wife съпруга *suprooga*
wild див *deef*
wind вятър *vyatur*
window прозорец *prozorets*; **in the shop window** на витрината *na vitreenata*
windscreen предно стъкло *predno stuklo*
windsurfing каране на сърф *karaneh na surf*
wine вино *veeno*
winter зима *zeema*
with с/със *s/sus*
withdraw тегля/да изтегля *teglya/da isteglya*
withdrawal теглене *tegleneh*
without без *bes*
woman жена *zhena*
wonderful чудесно *choodesno*
wood гора *gora*; *(material)* дърво *durvo*
wool вълна *vulna*
word дума *dooma*
work *(noun)* работа *rabota*; **work of art** произведение на изкуството *pro-izvedeni-eh na iskoostvoto*
work *(v)* работя *rabotya*
works: road works ремонт на пътя *remont na putya*
world свят *sfyat*
worse по-лош *po-losh*; **to get worse** влошава се *vloshava se*; **it's worse (than)** по-лошо е (от) *po-losho eh (ot)*
worth: to be worth струва *stroova*; **it's worth it** струва си *stroova see*
wound рана *rana*
wrist китка *keetka*
write пиша/да напиша *peesha/da napeesha* **13, 38**
wrong невярно *nevyarno*, неправилно *nepravilno*

XYZ

X-rays рентген *rentgen*

year година *godeena*
yellow жълт *zhult*
yes да *da*
yesterday вчера *fchera*; **yesterday evening** снощи *snoshti*
yet: not yet още не *oshteh neh*
you ти *tee (sing)*, вие *vee-eh (pl)*
young млад *mlat*
your твоят *tvo-yat*
yours твой *tvoy*
youth hostel туристическа спалня *tooristeecheska spalnya*, общежитие *opshtezheeti-eh*

zero нула *noola*
zip цип *tseep*
zoo зоологическа градина *zo-ologeecheska gradeena*
zoom (lens) зум леща *zoom leshta*

DICTIONARY

BULGARIAN-ENGLISH

Аа

авариен изход emergency exit
август August
авиокомпания airline
автокаско comprehensive car insurance
автобус bus; coach; **автобусна спирка** bus stop
автогара bus station
адаптор adaptor
адвокат (m), **адвокатка** (f) lawyer
дминистраторка (f) receptionist, **администратор** (m)
адрес address
аз I
акваланг wetsuit
ако if
акумулатор car battery
акцент accent
алангле rare (meat)
аларма alarm
алергичен allergic; **аз съм алергичен към ...** I'm allergic to ...
алея за велосипедисти cycle path
алкохол alcohol
алуминиево фолио tinfoil
американец (m), **американка** (f) American (noun)
американски American (adj)
английски English (adj)
англичанин (m), **англичанка** (f) English person
Англия England
антибиотик antibiotics
антракт interval (in play, film)
апартамент apartment, flat
апендисит appendicitis
април April
аптека chemist's
асансьор lift
аспирин aspirin
астма asthma
ауспух exhaust pipe

Бб

бавен slow
багаж luggage
багажник car boot
бакшиш tip
балкон balcony
банка bank
банкнота banknote
банкомат cashpoint
бански (костюм) swimming trunks; swimsuit
баня bathroom
бар bar
барбекю barbecue
басейн swimming pool
батерия battery
баща father
бебе baby
бебешко шише baby's bottle
беден poor
бедро thigh
без without; **без мито** tax-free; **без намаление** full fare, full price
безалкохолно fizzy drink
безглутенов gluten-free
безопасност safety
безплатен free (of charge)
безпокоя to disturb; **не ме безпокойте** do not disturb
безсъние insomnia
бележка note
бележник notebook
бельо underwear
беля/да обеля to peel
бензин petrol
бензиностанция petrol station
библиотека library
бижута jewellery
бижутерски магазин jeweller's
билет ticket; **билетът важи за ...** the ticket is valid for ...
билетен център ticket office

бинокъл binoculars
благодарение: благодарение на thanks to
благодарности thanks
благодаря to thank; **благодаря ти/ви** thank you; **много ти/ви благодаря** thank you very much
бланка form (document)
близо near; **близо до плажа** near the beach
близък close, near; **най-близкият ...** the nearest ...
блокиран, блокирал blocked
блуза sweater
бой fight
бойлер water heater
боклук rubbish
болен ill
болест illness
боли it hurts; **боли ме гърло(то)** I have a sore throat; **боли ме глава(та)** my head hurts
болница hospital
ботаническа градина botanical garden
ботуш boot
брава lock
брада beard
брадичка chin
брат brother
бременна pregnant
брой number; cash; **плащам в брой/да платя в брой** to pay cash
бронхит bronchitis
броня bumper
брошура brochure
броя to count
бръснарско ножче razor blade
бръснач razor
бряг coast; shore
будилник alarm clock
буря storm
бутам/да бутна to push
бутилка bottle; **газова бутилка** gas cylinder
бушон fuse
бъбрек kidney
бърз fast
бързам to be in a hurry
бързо quickly, fast
бял white
бял дроб lung
бяло вино white wine

Вв

в at/in; **в Англия** in England; **в чужбина** abroad; **в случай на ...** in case of ...; **в безопасност** safe
важен important
вали (дъжд) to rain; it's raining; **вали сняг** to snow; it's snowing
валиден valid
валута currency
вана bath
ваучер voucher; top-up card
вдругиден the day after tomorrow
вегетарианец (m), **вегетарианка** (f) vegetarian
веднага right; right away
веднъж: веднъж на ден/веднъж на всеки час once a day/an hour
век century
Великден Easter
Великобритания Great Britain
велосипед bicycle
веро washing-up liquid
вероятно probably
вестник newspaper
вече already
вечер evening; **вечерта** in the evening
вечерям to have dinner
вещ item
вземам/да взема to take; **вземам назаем/да взема назаем** to borrow
вземам под наем/да взема под наем to rent
вид sort
виждам/да видя to see
виза visa
вила villa
вилица fork
винаги always
вино wine
висок tall; high
витрина shop window; **на витрината** in the window
включвам/да включа to switch on; **включвам в контакта** to plug in
включен switched on; included
включително including
вкус flavour; taste; **има вкус на ...** it tastes of ...
вкъщи at home; **отивам си вкъщи** to go home; **за вкъщи** takeaway

влажен damp
влак train; влакът за София the train to Sofia
влизам/да вляза to come in; to go in
вместо instead; instead of
внимание attention; внимавай! watch out!
вода water
водопроводчик plumber
водоустойчив waterproof
волейбол volleyball
врат neck
врата door
време weather; time; времето е лошо the weather's bad; колко време? how long?
временен temporary
връзка tie; connection
връх top; summit; на върха at the top
връщам (се)/да (се) върна to return; to come back; to get back; to give back; връщам/да върна парите to refund
връщане return; билет за отиване и връщане return ticket
все едно all the same
всеки (m), всяка (f), всяко (n) each, every; everybody, everyone; всеки ден every day
всекидневна living room
всички all
всъщност in fact
втори second; втора класа second class; втора ръка second-hand
вторник Tuesday
вуйчо uncle
вход entrance; admission charge
вчера yesterday
възглавница pillow
въздух air
въздушна поща airmail
възможен possible
възможност opportunity
възпаление infection
възраст age
възрастен elderly
вълна wool
вън outside
въпреки че although
въпрос question
вървя пеша to walk
вътре inside

вярвам/да повярвам to believe
вярно true
вятър wind

Гг

гади ми се to feel sick
газ gas
газиран fizzy; газирана вода sparkling water
галерия gallery
гара train station
гараж garage
гаранция guarantee
гардероб cloakroom; left-luggage (office); wardrobe
гася/да изгася to extinguish
гащи pants
гей gay
гинеколог gynaecologist
гипс plaster cast
глава head
главен main
глад hunger
гладен съм to be hungry
гледам to look at
глезен ankle
глоба fine (noun)
глух deaf
гмуркам се to dive
гмуркане diving
говоря to talk, to speak; говорете по-високо! speak up!
годен до best before
годеник fiancé
годеница fiancée
година year
годишнина anniversary
голф golf; голф игрище golf course
голям big
гора forest; wood
горе above
горещ hot; горещо е it's hot
горещина heat
господин Mr; господине sir
госпожа Mrs; госпожо madam
госпожица Miss; госпожице miss
гост (m), гостенка (f) guest
гостоприемство hospitality; welcome
готвене cooking

готвя to cook
готов ready
град town; city; **градски транспорт** public transport
градина garden
градус degree
грам gram
гребен comb
грешка mistake; **правя грешка** to make a mistake
грижа се за to look after
грил barbecue
грип flu
гробища cemetery
група group
гръб back; **на гърба на** at the back of
губя/да загубя to lose; **да се загубя** to get lost; **загубих се** I'm lost
гума tyre
гъба sponge
гълтам/да глътна to swallow
гърди chest
гърло throat

Дд

да yes
да изгоря to get sunburn
да проявя филм to get a film developed
да доведа някого to go and fetch someone; **да донеса нещо** to go and fetch something
давам/да дам to give; **давам/да дам назаем** to lend; **давам под наем/да дам под наем** to rent out
давя се/да се удавя to drown
далече far; **далече от** far from
дали whether
данък tax
дата date (noun); **дата на раждане** date of birth
датира (от) to date (from)
два two; both; **и двата** (m)/**и двете** (f) both of us; **и двамата** (m)/**и двете** (f) both
движение traffic
двоен double
двойка pair
дворец palace
дебитна карта debit card

ДДС VAT
дежурна аптека duty chemist's
дезинфекцирам to disinfect
дезодорант deodorant
декември December
декларирам to declare
ден day
денонощен 24-hour
депозит deposit
десен right (adj)
десерт dessert
дестинация destination
дете child; **деца** children
дефект flaw
дефектен damaged
джамия mosque
джапанки flip-flops
джогинг jogging
диабет diabetes
диапозитив slide (noun)
див wild
дизел diesel
директен direct
дискотека disco
днес today
до beside; **до поискване** poste restante; **до(като)** until; **до утре!** see you tomorrow!
добавка supplement
добре fine (adv); **добре съм** I'm fine; **добре опечено** well done (meat); **още по-добре** all the better; **добре дошли!** welcome!
добър good; **добро утро** good morning; **добър ден** good afternoon; **добър вечер** good evening; **добър апетит!** enjoy your meal!
довечера tonight; this evening
довиждане goodbye
доволен pleased
докато while
докосвам/да докосна to touch
документи за самоличност identity papers
долина valley
дом home; **у дома** at home
домакинска работа housework
допълнителен extra
доста quite a lot of
достатъчно enough
достъп access

дрехи clothes
друг another; other
дума word
душ shower; **вземам душ** to take a shower
душгел shower gel
души: за колко души? for how many people?
дъжд rain
дълбок deep
дължа to owe
дълъг long; **дълго** a long time; **много дълго** for ages
дъно bottom; **на дъното на** at the bottom of
дърво wood; tree
държа to hold
държава state
дърпам/да дръпна to pull
дъска board
дъщеря daughter
дюшек mattress

Ее

Европа Europe
европейски European
евтин cheap
един (m), **една** (f), **едно** (n) a; one
единичен single
еднократен: за еднократна употреба disposable
езеро lake
език language; tongue
екологичен ecological, organic
екскурзия trip
екскурзовод guide
експресен express (adj)
еластична лепенка Elastoplast®
електрически electric; **електрическа самобръсначка** electric shaver
електричество electricity
електромер electricity meter
епилептик (m), **епилептичка** (f) epileptic
есемес text message
есен autumn
етаж storey; floor

Жж

жаден thirsty
жалко it's a pity
жена woman; **жени** ladies (toilet)
женен (m) married
жепе гара train station
жив alive
живея to live
живот life
животно animal
жилетка cardigan
жълт yellow

Зз

за for; **за един час** for an hour
забавен fun
забележителност landmark
заболяване condition (medical)
забравям/да забравя to forget
забранен forbidden
зависи (от) it depends (on)
загуба на съзнание blackout
зад behind
задавам/да задам въпрос to ask a question
задръстване traffic jam
заедно together
зает occupied; busy; **всичко е заето** everything's full
заето engaged (toilet)
заключвам/да заключа to lock
закусвам/да закуся to have breakfast
закуска breakfast; snack
закъсвам/да закъсам to break down
закъснение delay; **със закъснение** delayed
закъснявам/да закъснея to be late
залез sunset
заминавам/да замина to go away; **заминаваме си утре** we're going home tomorrow
заминаване departure
занимавам се I play; I do (as hobby or profession); **занимавам се с рекламата** I work in advertising
запад west; **на запад** in the west; **на запад от** to the west of
запазвам/да запазя to book, to reserve;

(on computer) to save
запазен reserved
запалвам/да запала to light
запалка lighter
запечен roasted; constipated
заповядай(те) here you are; come in; take a seat
запомням/да запомня to remember
започвам/да започна to begin
заразен contagious
зареждам/да заредя (отново) to recharge
застраховка insurance
затварям/да затворя to close
затворено closed
затова therefore
защо why; **няма защо** you're welcome
защото because
звъня/да звънна to ring
здраве health
здравей *(sg)*, **здравейте** *(pl)* hello
здрасти hi!
зелен green
зеленчук vegetable
земя ground; earth; **на земята** on the ground
зима winter
зимен курорт ski resort
злополука accident
знак sign
знам to know; **не знам** I don't know
знача to mean; **какво значи ...?** what does … mean?
зона area
зоологическа градина zoo
зрял ripe
зум zoom (lens)
зъб tooth
зъболекар dentist

Ии

и and
играя to play
игрище sports ground
идвам/да дойда to come
избирам/да избера to select
извинение excuse
извинявам се/да се извиня to excuse oneself; **извинявай** *(sg)*, **извинявайте**

(pl) excuse me, sorry
използвам to use; **да се използва за** to be used for
изгарям (се)/да (се) изгоря to burn (oneself)
изгаряне burn
изглед view; **изглед към морето** sea view
изглеждам to seem; to look
изгрев sunrise
изгоряло burnt
изкарвам/да изкарам to spend *(time)*
изкачвам се/да се изкача to go up, to climb
изключвам/да изключа to switch off
изкуство art; **произведение на изкуството** work of art
изкълчвам/да изкълча to sprain; **изкълчвам/да изкълча глезена си** to sprain one's ankle
излизам/да изляза to go out; to come out
излитам/да излетя to take off *(plane)*
излишък excess
изложба exhibition
измервателен уред meter
изморен exhausted
изнасилване rape
изпращам/да изпратя to see home
изпускам/да изпусна to miss; **изпуснахме влака** we missed the train
изпълвам/да изпълня to fill out
изразявам/да изразя to express
изречение sentence
изсушавам/да изсуша to dry
изток east; **на изток** in the east; **на изток от** (to the) east of
изтривам/да изтрия to delete
изхвърлям/да изхвърля to throw out; **изхвърлям/да изхвърля боклука** to take the rubbish out
изход exit; gate
изчерпан out of stock
или or
има there is/are
имам to have; **имам диария** to have diarrhoea
име first name
имейл (адрес) e-mail (address)
имунизиран срещу vaccinated against
иначе otherwise

инвалид disabled person
инвалидна количка wheelchair
инжекция injection
инсектицид insecticide
интернет Internet
интернет кафе Internet café
инфаркт heart attack
инфекция infection
информация information
Ирландия Ireland
ирландски Irish
искам to want; **искам да направя нещо** to want to do something; **искам да кажа** I mean

Кк

кабелна телевизия cable television
кавга fight
казвам се to be called
казвам/да кажа to tell; **как се казва ...?** how do you say...?; **казват, че ...** they say that ...
как how; **как си** *(sg)* **/сте** *(pl)* **?** how are you?
какво what; **какво искате?** what do you want?
както as; **както и да е** anyway
какъв вид ...? what kind of ...?
калъфка за възглавница pillowcase
камион lorry
камък stone
кана jug
канал channel
кану каяк kayak
каня/да поканя to invite
капак cover *(noun)*
капки drops
каравана caravan
карам to drive
каране на водни ски waterskiing
каране на ски skiing; **отивам да карам ски** to go skiing
каране на сърф windsurfing; **отивам да карам сърф** to go surfing
карта map; card; **лична карта** identity card; **картичка** business card
картина painting
каса ticket office
каска helmet

катастрофа (car) accident
катедрала cathedral
катерене climbing
като like; as; **щом като** as soon as
кафе coffee
кафене café
кафяв brown
качвам се/да се кача to go up
качване boarding
качество quality; **с добро/лошо качество** of good/bad quality
кашлица cough; **имам кашлица** I have a cough
кашлям to cough
квартира accommodation
кей quay
килим(че) carpet
километър kilometre
кино cinema
китка wrist
клапан stopcock
климат climate
климатик air conditioning
ключ key
книга book
книжарница bookshop
кога when
когато when
код code; **код за влизане** door code; **телефонен код** dialling code
кожа skin
козметика toiletries
кой who; which; **кой се обажда?** who's calling?
който who
кола car
кола Coke®
колекция collection
колело bike; wheel; **планинско колело** mountain bike
колет parcel
количка pram; pushchair
колко how much?; **колкото може по-бързо** as soon as possible
коловоз platform
коляно knee
комар mosquito
компания company
компютър computer
консерва tin, can
консулство consulate

контакт socket; contact
контактни лещи contact lenses
концерт concert; **концертна зала** concert hall
копие copy
копирам to copy
кораб boat; ship
коса hair
котлон hotplate
кошче bin; **кошче за боклук** dustbin
крада/да открадна to steal
крадец thief
кражба theft
край end; **край на работното време** closing time; **в края на** at the end of
крак leg; foot
кран tap
красив beautiful
кредитна карта credit card
крем cream; **крем за бръснене** shaving cream; **слънцезащитен крем** suncream
круиз cruise
крушка light bulb
кръв blood
кръвно налягане blood pressure; **високо кръвно налягане** high blood pressure; **ниско кръвно налягане** low blood pressure
кръгово движение roundabout
кръгъл round
кръст cross
кубче лед ice cubes
купа bowl
купе compartment
купон party
купувам/да купя to buy
курорт resort; holiday camp; spa
курс exchange rate
кутия box
куфар suitcase
кухня kitchen
къде where; **къде е/са ...?** where is/are ...?; **откъде си/сте?** where are you from?; **къде отиваш?** where are you going?
където where
към towards; about
къмпинг campsite; **ходя на къмпинг** to go camping
къмпингар camper
къмпингов котлон camping stove

къпя се/да се окъпя to have a bath/ shower
кърпа towel; **кърпа за лице** facecloth
къс short
късмет luck
късно late; **късно е** it's late
къща house

Лл

лампа lamp
лаптоп laptop
легло bed
лед ice
лек light *(adj)*
лека нощ goodnight
лекар doctor
лекарски кабинет surgery
лекарство medicine
лепенка sticking plaster; Sellotape®
лесен easy
летище airport
летя to fly
леща lens; **лещи** lenses
лилав purple
линейка ambulance
линия line; **линия на метрото** underground line
липсва to be missing; **липсват два/две ...** there are two ... missing
лира pound (sterling)
листовка leaflet
листчета за цигари cigarette paper
литър litre
лице face
лична карта identity card
лодка fishing boat
лош bad; **не е лошо** it's not bad
луна парк funfair
лъжица spoon
любим favourite
любител fan
ляв left; **наляво/вляво (от)** to the left (of)
лято summer

Мм

магазин shop; **магазин за цигари** tobacconist's

магистрала motorway
мазнина fat
май May
майка mother
малко few; little *(adv)*
малък little, small
манастир monastery
маратонка training shoe
марка stamp
март March
маршрут route; bus route
маса table
масло oil
материал material
маунтин байк mountain bike
махам/да махна to get off
мебелиран furnished
меден месец honeymoon
медицински спирт surgical spirit
между between
международен international
мене me
менструация periods
меню menu
месарница butcher's
месец month
местен local; **местно време** local time
метро underground, tube
метър metre
мигач indicator
мида shellfish
микровълнова печка microwave
минавам/да мина to pass
минал past *(adj)*; **миналата година** last year
минало past *(noun)*
минерална вода mineral water
минута minute; **в последната минута** at the last minute
миризма smell
мириша to smell
мисля (за/че) to think (about/that)
митница customs
мишка mouse
мия (се)/да (се)измия to (have a) wash; **да си измия косата** to wash one's hair
миялна машина dishwasher
млад young
много a lot (of); very; many
мобилен телефон mobile (phone)
мога to be able to; **не мога** I can't

модерен modern
може би maybe, perhaps; **може да вали** it might rain
мой mine
мокър wet
молив pencil
моля please
моля? pardon?
момент moment; **в момента** at the moment
моминско име maiden name
момиче girl
момче boy
монета coin
море sea
морски sea; **морски курорт** seaside resort; **морски специалитети** seafood; **морска болест** seasickness
мост bridge
мотопед moped
мотор engine; motorbike
мравка ant
мразя to hate
мрежа gauze
мръсен dirty *(adj)*
музей museum
музика music; **музика на живо** live music
мускул muscle
муха fly
мъж man; **мъже** gents' (toilet)
мълчалив silent
място place; space; seat

Нн

на of; per; at; away; in; **на нас** ours; **на човек** per person; **дават го в ...** it's on at ...; **на море** at the seaside; **на два километра** two kilometres away; **на български** in Bulgarian
навън outside
набирам/да набера to dial
наблюдавам to watch
навреме on time
навсякъде everywhere
надясно (от) to the right (of)
наем rent; **под наем** for hire
наемам/да наема to hire
наемател *(m)*, **наемателка** *(f)* tenant

наздраве! cheers!
най-големият the most
най-добър best; **най-добрият** the best
найлонов плик plastic bag
най-малък the least
най-накрая finally
наливна бира draught beer
намаление reduction, discount
намалявам/да намаля to reduce
намирам/да намеря to find
напитка drink
напомням/да напомня to remind
напоследък recently
направо straight ahead, straight on
напред forward
напускам/да напусна to leave; to check out
напълвам/да напълня to fill up
наркотици drugs
народни танци folk dancing
нарочно on purpose
нарязан sliced
насекомо insect
настанявам/да настаня to put up (for the night)
настинка cold *(noun)*; **настинал съм** to have a cold
натиск pressure
национален празник national holiday
начало beginning; **в началото** at the beginning
начинаещ beginner
наш our; ours
не no; not; **не, благодаря** no, thank you; **още не** not yet
небе sky
невъзможен impossible
невярно wrong
него him
негов his
неделя Sunday
необходим necessary
непитейна вода non-drinking water
непосредствено до right beside
неправилно wrong
непушач non-smoker
нескафе instant coffee
неудобен uncomfortable
нещо anything; something; **нещо друго** something else
нея, неин her

ние we
никакъв none; not any
никога never
никой nobody
никъде nowhere
нисък low
нито neither; **нито ... нито ...** neither ... nor ...
нищо nothing
но but
нов new; **Нова година** New Year
новини news
ноември November
нож knife
ножица scissors
нокът nail
номер number
нос nose
носна кърпа handkerchief
нося to wear; to carry
нося/да донеса to bring
нощ night
нощен клуб nightclub
нула zero
някакъв some
някога once
някой anybody, anyone; somebody, someone
няколко several; **няколко души** some people
някъде somewhere; **някъде другаде** somewhere else
няма there is/are not
нямам not to have; **няма значение** it doesn't matter; **нямам нищо против** I don't mind; **нямам представа** no idea

Oo

обаждам се/да се обадя (по телефона) to phone
обаждане call
обед midday; lunch
Обединеното кралство United Kingdom
обектив lens
обеци earrings
обещавам/да обещая to promise
обикновено usually
обиколка с екскурзовод guided tour

обличам се/да се облека to get dressed
обменно бюро bureau de change
обменям/да обменя to exchange money
обмяна exchange
оборудване equipment
обратен opposite *(adj)*
обръщам (се)/да (се) обърна to turn
обувки shoes
обувки за ски ski boots
общ general, common, shared
обществен public
община town hall
обяд lunch
обядвам to have lunch
огледало mirror
огън fire; **имате ли огънче?** have you got a light?
одеало blanket
оживен busy
океан ocean
окей OK
око eye
около around; about
октомври October
омръзна (ми) to be fed up (with)
омъжена *(f)* married
онези those
онзи that
оня ден the day before yesterday
опакован packed
опасен dangerous
опасност danger
опашка queue
оперирам to operate
опитвам/да опитам to taste
опитвам се/да се опитам to try
оплаквам се/да се оплача to complain
оправям се/да се оправя to get by
оптик optician
организирам to organize
ордьовър hors d'oeuvres; starter
оркестър band; orchestra
оса wasp
освен except; beside
осигурен provided; insured
основен basic
оставам/да остана to stay; to remain
останалите the rest
останки ruins
остров island

от from; since; **от ... до ...** from … to…
отбор team
отварям/да отворя to open
отварячка bottle opener; **отварячка за консерви** can opener
отворен open; **отворено до късно** late-night opening
от време навреме from time to time
отговарям/да отговоря to reply, to answer
отговор reply, answer
отдавна a long time ago
отделен separate
отделение department; ward
отделно separately
отдолу below
отивам/да отида to go; **отивам да поплувам** to go for a swim; **отивам на разходка** to go for a walk; **отивам с** to go with; **отивам в София/България** to go to Sofia/to Bulgaria
отиване: билет за отиване single ticket
отказвам/да откажа to refuse
откакто since
открит open-air; **открит лифт** chairlift; **на открито** in the open
отлив low tide
отменям to cancel
отнемам/да отнема to take away; **отнема два часа** it takes two hours
отопление heating
отпадъци waste
офис office
официален празник public holiday
охрана security
очевиден obvious
очила glasses
още still; **още не** not yet

Пп

павилион newsstand; kiosk
падам/да падна to fall
пазар market
пазаруване shopping; **пазарувам/да напазарувам** to do some/the shopping
пазя/да запазя to keep; to care for; to look after
пак again
пакет packet

палатка tent
паля/да запаля to light
паметник monument
памук cotton wool
памучен cotton; памучна клечка cotton bud
панаир fair (n)
панталон trousers
параклис chapel
пари money
паричен превод transfer (of money)
парк park
паркинг car park
паркирам to park
партер ground floor
парти party
партньор partner
парче bit; piece
паспорт passport
паста за зъби toothpaste
пациент (m), пациентка (f) patient
пейзаж landscape; scenery
пека се на слънце to sunbathe
пека/да изпека to bake, to roast
пелена nappy
пепелник ashtray
пера/да изпера to do the washing
пералня washing machine; launderette
перон platform
петно stain
петък Friday
пеша on foot
пешеходец pedestrian
пешеходна зона pedestrianized street
пиеса play
пикантен spicy
пикник picnic
пин код PIN (number)
писалка pen
писмо letter
питам/да попитам to ask
питие drink (n)
пиша/да напиша to write; to type; как се пише? how do you spell it?
пишкам to pee
пия/да изпия to drink
плавам to sail
плаж beach
плажна шапка sunhat
плакат poster
план plan

планина mountain
пластмасов plastic
платноходство sailing
плача to cry
плащам/да платя to pay
плик envelope
плод и зеленчук grocer's
пломба filling (in tooth)
плосък flat (adj)
площад square
плувам to swim
плуване swimming
побързай! (sg), побързайте! (pl) hurry (up)!
повече more; any more; повечето хора most people; повече от more than; няма повече there's no more
повреда breakdown
повръщам/да повърна to vomit
повтарям/да повторя to repeat
под under; underneath
подарък present
подател sender
подводен спорт scuba diving
по-добър better
подписвам/да подпиша to sign
подправка spice
подреден tidy
подут swollen
подходящ suitable
пожар! fire!
пожарна команда fire brigade
познавам/да позная to recognize
показвам/да покажа to show
покрай past (prep)
покривам/да покрия to cover
по-късно later
пол sex
пола skirt
полет flight
полицай (m), полицайка (f) policeman, policewoman
полицейско управление police station
полиция police
половин half; половин литър/кило half a litre/kilo; половин час half an hour; час и половина an hour and a half
по-лош worse; по-лошо е (от) it's worse (than)
полунощ midnight
полупансион half-board

получавам/да получа to receive; to get
помагам/да помогна to help
по-малко less; по-малко от less than
помощ help; помощ! help!; викам
 помощ to call for help
помпа pump
поне at least
понеделник Monday
понякога sometimes; occasionally
попълвам/да попълня to fill in
поради because of
портмоне purse
портокал orange
портфейл wallet
порязвам се/да се порежа to cut oneself
поръчвам/да поръчам to order
поръчка order
посещавам/да посетя to visit
посещение visit
последен final, last
посока direction
посолство embassy
посребрен silver-plated
пот sweat
потвърждавам/да потвърдя to
 confirm
почивам си/да си почина to rest
почивка rest; nap; holiday; на почивка
 on holiday
почти almost; почти никак hardly any
поща post; post office
пощальон postman
пощенска картичка postcard
пощенска кутия letterbox
пощенски код postcode
правилен correct
право right (noun); имам правото да ...
 to have the right to ...
правя/да направя to make; to do
празен empty
празненство celebration
празник, празници holiday(s)
практичен practical
прах за пране washing powder
пращам/да пратя to send
превеждам/да преведа to translate
превод translation; паричен превод
 money order
превръзка bandage
предварително in advance
пред in front of

преди before
предишен former; previous
предлагам/да предложа to offer; to
 suggest; to propose
предмет object, thing
предна част front
предно стъкло windscreen
предпазвам/да предпазя to protect
предпазен колан safety belt
предпочитам/да предпочета to prefer
предупреждавам/да предупредя
 to warn
предястие starter
през during; across; през деветнайсети
 век in the 19th century; през уикенда
 over the weekend
презерватив condom
прекалено too; too much; прекалено
 много too much/too many
прекачвам се/да се прекача to change
 (vehicle)
прекрасен lovely
премахвам/да премахна to remove
премествам се/да се преместя to
 move to
препарат за миене на съдове
 washing-up liquid
препечен toasted
препоръчвам/да препоръчам to
 recommend; препоръчано писмо
 registered letter
пресичам to cross
преследвам to follow
престой stay
претъпкан packed
прехвърлям (се)/да (се)прехвърля
 to transfer
приготвям/да приготвя to prepare
приемам to accept
прилив high tide
примирявам се/да се примиря to
 put up with
припадам/да припадна to faint
природа nature
приспивателно sleeping pill
пристанище port; яхтено пристанище
 marina
пристигам/да пристигна to arrive
пристигане arrival
притежавам to own
притеснен nervous

пришка blister
приятел *(m)*, **приятелка** *(f)* friend; boyfriend/ girlfriend
приятен pleasant; nice; **приятно ми е!** pleased to meet you!
пробвам to try on
проблем problem
пробна fitting room
проверка check; control
проверявам/да проверя to check
прогноза forecast; **прогноза за времето** weather forecast
програма programme; listings magazine
продава се for sale
продавам/да продам to sell; **продаден** sold out
продавач *(m)*, **продавачка** *(f)* shop assistant
продукт product
продължавам to continue, to proceed; **продължавайте да** to keep doing
прозорец window; **прозорци със стъклопис** stained-glass windows
пролет spring
против against
противозачатъчно contraceptive; **вземам противозачатъчни** to be on the pill
професия profession
прохладен cool
пропуск pass
процент percent
процесия procession
пръст finger
пръстен ring
пряк direct; **пряк път** short cut
пудра powder
пукам/да спукам to burst
пура cigar
пуша to smoke; **пушенето забранено** no smoking
пушач smoker
пчела bee
пълен full; **пълен пансион** full board; **пълна застраховка** comprehensive insurance; **пълен с** full of
пълня to fill
пъпка spot *(on face)*
първи first; **първа класа** first class; **първи етаж** first floor; **първо** first (of all)

пържа/да изпържа to fry
пържен fried
пързалям се to slide
път road; way; time; **приятен път!** have a good trip!; **три/четири пъти** three/ four times
пътеводител guidebook
пътека path
пътен road; **пътен знак** roadsign; **пътна помощ** breakdown service; **пътна такса** toll
пътник passenger
пътнически чек traveller's cheque
пътувам to travel; **пътувам на стоп** to hitchhike
пътуване journey
пясък sand

Рр

работа job; work; occupation
работя to work; **не работи** out of order
радиатор radiator
радио radio
радиостанция radio station
разбирам/да разбера to understand; **разбира се** of course
разболявам се/да се разболея to fall ill
развалини ruins; **разрушен** in ruins
развалям се/да се разваля to break down
разговор conversation
разговорник phrasebook
разлика difference; **разлика във времето** time difference
различен (от) different (from)
размер size
разписание timetable
разписка receipt
разпродажба sales; **на разпродажба** in the sale
разтревожен upset
разумен reasonable
разхождам се/да се разходя to walk
район area; **в този район** in the area
ракета racket
рамо shoulder
рана wound
ранен injured
раница backpack, rucksack

рано early
расист racist
раста/да порасна to grow
растение plant
ребро rib
ревматизъм rheumatism
регистрационен номер registration number
регистрация check-in
регистрирам се to check in; to register
регистриран registered
ред turn; **твой ред е** (sg), **ваш ред е** (pl) it's your turn
режа/да нарежа to cut
резервен spare; **резервна гума** spare tyre; **резервна част** spare part; **резервно колело** spare wheel
резервоар tank
река river
ремарке trailer
ремонт на пътя road works
ремонтирам to repair
рентген X-rays
ресто change (money)
ресторант restaurant; **ресторант за бърза закуска** fast-food restaurant
рецепта prescription; recipe
рецепция reception; **на рецепцията** at reception
риба fish
рибен магазин fish shop
риза shirt
родители parents
рожден ден birthday
розе rosé wine
розов pink
роман novel
ръка arm; hand
ръчен hand-made; **ръчен багаж** hand luggage; **ръчна спирачка** handbrake
рядко rarely, seldom
рядък rare

Cc

с with; by; **с къси ръкави** short-sleeved; **с намаление** at a discount; **с тен** tanned; **с кола** by car
салфетка napkin
само only, just

самобръсначка shaver
самолет aeroplane
сандали sandals
сантиметър centimetre
сапун soap
светкавица flash; lightning
светлина light
светофар traffic lights
светъл light (adj); **светлосин** light blue
свещ candle
свещи spark plugs
свикнал съм (m), **свикнала съм** (f) I'm used to it
свободен free; vacant
свой one's own
свръхбагаж excess luggage
свършвам/да свърша to finish
свят world
сготвен cooked
сграда building
себе си himself; myself
север north; **на север** in the north; **на север от** (to the) north of
сега now; nowadays
седмица week
сезон season
село village
семеен лекар GP
семейство family
сенна хрема hay fever
септември September
сервирам to serve
сервитьор (m), **сервитьорка** (f) waiter, waitress
сериозен serious
сестра sister; nurse
сешоар hairdrier
сив grey
сигнал signal
сигурен sure; secure
сиди CD
силен strong; loud
син blue
син son
синагога synagogue
сироп syrup
скала cliff; rock
скара grill; barbecue
ски ski; **ски влек** drag lift; **ски лифт** ski lift
скоро soon; **до скоро!** see you soon!;

скоро ще ... to be about to ...
скорост speed
скоростна кутия gearbox
скоч scotch *(whisky)*; Sellotape®
скутер scooter
скъп dear, expensive
слаб weak
слагам/да сложа to put
сладък sweet *(adj)*
след after; **след един час** in an hour
следвам to follow
следване studies
следващ next
следобед afternoon
слизам/да сляза to go down
случай: за всеки случай just in case
случва се to happen
слушам to listen
слънце sun; **на слънце** in the sun
слънцезащитен крем sun cream
слънчев удар sunstroke
слънчеви очила sunglasses
сляп blind
сменям/да сменя to change
сметка account; bill; **за тяхна сметка** reverse-charge call
смея се to laugh
снимам някого to take someone's photo; **снимам нещо** to take a photo (of)
снимка photo
снощи yesterday evening; last night
сняг snow
собствен own *(adj)*; **собствената ми кола** my own car
собственик *(m)*, **собственичка** *(f)* owner
сок juice
сол salt
солен salty
спален чувал sleeping bag
спасявам/да спася to save
специален special
специалитет speciality; **специалитетът за деня** today's special
спешен urgent; **спешен случай** emergency
спирала coil *(contraceptive)*
спирам/да спра to stop; to brake
спирачка brake
спирка stop
списание magazine

спомням си/да си спомня to recall
според according to
спорт sport
справки inquiries
спукан burst *(adj)*; **спукана гума** flat tyre
спя to sleep; **спи ми се** to be sleepy; **спя с** to sleep with
сребро silver
сред among
среда middle; **в средата (на)** in the middle (of)
среден medium
среща meeting; appointment
срещам (се)/да (се) срещна to meet; **да се срещна с** to have a meeting with
срещу against; opposite *(prep)*
срок на годност expiry date
сряда Wednesday
ставам/да стана to get up
стадион stadium
станция на метрото underground station
стар old; **стари хора** old people; **стария град** the old town; **на старо** second hand
старомоден out of date
стая room
степен degree
стигам/да стигна to reach; **стига!** that's enough!
стил style
стоки goods
стол chair
стомах stomach
стомашен грип gastric flu
страдам to suffer
страна country; side
страхотен great
строя/да построя to build
струва worth; cost; **струва си** it's worth it; **колко струва?** how much does it cost?
студен cold *(adj)*; **студено е** it's cold; **студено ми е** I'm cold
студент *(m)*, **студентка** *(f)* student
стълби stairs
стъпка step
субтитри subtitles
сувенир souvenir
сума amount
супена лъжица tablespoon

супермаркет supermarket
суров raw
сутрин morning
сух dry *(adj)*
счупване fracture
счупен broken
събарям/да съборя to knock down
съблекалня changing room
събота Saturday
събуждам се/да се събудя to wake up
съвет advice
съветвам to advise
съвсем quite
съвършен perfect
съд vessel; **съдове** dishes
Съединените щати United States
съединител clutch
съжалявам to be sorry
съм to be
сън sleep *(n)*
съобщавам/да съобщя to report
съобщение message
съпруг husband
съпруга wife
сърдечен удар heart attack
сърф surfboard; **карам сърф** to windsurf
сърце heart
съсед neighbour
състояние state
същият the same
също also
сядам/да седна to sit down; **седнете!** take a seat!
сянка shade; **на сянка** in the shade

Тт

табелка road sign; notice
таблетка tablet, pill
така so; **така, че** so that
такса tax; charge
такси taxi
талия waist
талон car-ownership document
там there; over there
тампон tampon
танц dance
танцувам to dance
тапи за уши earplugs

твой yours
твърд hard
твърде rather; too
те they
театър theatre
теглене withdrawal
тегля/да изтегля to withdraw
тежък heavy
тези these
телевизия television
телефон telephone
телефонен номер phone number
телефонен секретар answering machine
телефонистка switchboard operator
телефонна кабина phone box
телефонни услуги directory enquiries
температура temperature; **меря си температурата** to take one's temperature
тен tan
тенджера pot
тенис tennis
тенискорт tennis court
тераса terrace
терминал terminal
термометър thermometer
термос flask
тесен tight
техен theirs
ти you
тиган frying pan
тийнейджър *(m)*, **тийнейджърка** *(f)* teenager
тип type
тирбушон corkscrew
тих quiet; silent
то it
тоалетна toilet; **тоалетна хартия** toilet paper; **тоалетна чантичка** toilet bag
тогава then
този this
той he
току-що пристигнах I've just arrived
топка ball
топъл warm; **топла напитка** hot drink; **топъл шоколад** hot chocolate
тост toast
точен exact
точка point
травълър чек traveller's cheque
традиционен traditional

трае last; it lasts; **трайно ли е?** does it last?
трамвай tram
трафик traffic
трева grass
треска fever
треска splinter
тролей trolley bus
труден difficult
тръгвам/да тръгна to leave
трън thorn; splinter
трябва have to; **трябва да отида** I have to go
тук here
турист (*m*), **туристка** (*f*) tourist
туристическа агенция travel agency
туристическа класа economy class
туристическа спалня youth hostel
туристически информационен център tourist office
туристически обувки walking boots
тъжен sad
тъмен dark; **тъмносин** dark blue
тънък thin
търговски център shopping centre
търся to look for
тютюн tobacco
тя she
тяло body

Уу

убивам/да убия to kill
увеселителен парк theme park
уговарям/да уговоря to arrange; **уговарям среща с** to arrange to meet
удобен comfortable
удоволствие pleasure; **с удоволствие** I'd love to
уеб страница website
Уелс Wales
уелски Welsh
ужасен terrible
ужилвам/да ужиля to sting; **ужилен (съм)** (*m*), **ужилена (съм)** (*f*) to get stung (by)
ужилване sting (*n*)
уикенд weekend
указател directory
улица street

умивалник washbasin
умирам to die
уморен tired
умрял dead
унгвент ointment
универсален магазин department store
Уокман Walkman®
упойка anaesthetic
управител manager
управлявам to manage
урок lesson
услуга favour; **правя услуга на някого** to do someone a favour
успявам/да успея to manage
уста mouth
устна lip
утре tomorrow; **утре вечер** tomorrow evening; **утре сутринта** tomorrow morning
ухапвам/ да ухапя to bite
ухапване bite
ухо ear
уча/да науча to learn
уча to study
участвам to take part
училище school

Фф

факс fax
факт fact
фактура invoice
фамилно име surname
фар lighthouse; headlight
февруари February
фенерче torch
ферибот ferry
фестивал festival
филия slice
филм film
фойерверки fireworks
фонокарта phonecard
форма shape
формуляр form (*document*)
фотоапарат camera
фризер freezer
фризьор hairdresser
фурна oven
футбол soccer

Xx

хавлиена кърпа towel
хайде да let's
ханш hip
харесвам/да харесам to like
хартия paper; **хартиена кърпичка** paper tissue
харча/да похарча to spend *(money)*
хашиш hashish
хващам/да хвана to catch
хвърлям/да хвърля to throw
хижа mountain hut
химическо чистене dry cleaner's
хладен chilly
хладилник fridge
хладък lukewarm
хлебарка cockroach
хлебарница baker's
хляб bread
ходя to go; **ходя на концерт** to go to a concert; **ходя на планина** to go hiking; **ходя на ресторант** to eat out
ходене walking, hiking
хол living room
хомосексуалист homosexual
хора people
хотел hotel
храна food
хранително отравяне food poisoning
хрема cold; runny nose
хубав nice
художник *(m)*, **художничка** *(f)* artist
хълм hill

Цц

цвят colour; **цветна снимка** colour photo
цена price, cost; fare
център centre; **центъра на града** town centre
цигара cigarette
цирк circus
цифров фотоапарат digital camera
църква church
цял whole **цял ден** all day; **цяла седмица** all week **през цялото време** all the time

Чч

чадър umbrella; beach umbrella
чаена лъжичка teaspoon
чакайте hold on!, wait!
чакалня waiting room
чакам/да изчакам wait **чакам някого** to wait for somebody **чакам на опашка** to queue up
чанта bag
чао bye!
чаршаф sheet
час hour **колко е часът?** what time is it?; **имам час за** to have an appointment (with) **запазвам час** to make an appointment
част part
частен private
чаша glass; cup **чаша вода/вино** a glass of water/of wine
час hour; appointment
чело forehead
червен red; **червен светофар** red light; **червено вино** red wine
черга rug
черен black
черен дроб liver
черпя treat; **аз черпя** my treat
често often
чета/да прочета to read
четвърт quarter
четвъртък Thursday
четка brush; **четка за зъби** toothbrush
чий whose
чиния plate; **мия чиниите/да измия чиниите** to do the dishes
чист clean *(adj)*
чистя/да изчистя to clean
чифт pair
член member
човек person
чорапи socks; stockings
чорапогащи tights
чувам/да чуя to hear
чувствам (се) to feel
чувство feeling; sense
чудесно wonderful
чужд foreign
чужденец foreigner
чупливо fragile

чупя/да счупя to break; **да си счупя крака** to break one's leg

Шш

шампоан shampoo
шапка hat
широк wide
шлифер raincoat
шок shock
шокиращ shocking
шорти shorts
Шотландия Scotland
шотландски Scottish
шосе road
шоу show *(n)*
шофьор driver
шофьорска книжка driving licence
шум noise; **вдигам/да вдигна шум** to make a noise
шумно noisy

Щщ

щастлив happy
щека ski pole

Ъъ

ъгъл corner
-ът *(m)*, **-та** *(f)*, **-то** *(n)*, **-те** *(pl)* the

Юю

юг south; **на юг** in the south; **на юг от** (to the) south of
юли July
юни June
ютия iron

Яя

ядене meal
яздя to ride
яке jacket
ям/да изям to eat
януари January
ястие dish
ясно clear
яхта yacht

GRAMMAR

Talking about people and things

Gender of nouns

All nouns in Bulgarian should be referred to as *he, she* or *it*.

Masculine nouns as a rule end in a consonant (a hard sound) or in the semi-vowel **-й**:

мъж man	музей museum
лекар doctor	чай tea

Feminine nouns end in **-а** or **-я** (a soft sound):

жена woman	баня bathroom
маса table	ваканция holiday

Neuter nouns end in **-е** and **-о**, but in borrowed foreign words also in **-и**, **-у**, **-ю**:

куче dog	такси taxi	шоу show
село village	парти party	меню menu

Number and quantity

The masculine plural adds **-ове** to single syllable nouns and **-и** to nouns with more than one syllable:

стол – стол**ове**	лекар – лекар**и**
чай – чай**ове**	музей – музе**и**

To make the plural from feminine nouns the final **-а** or **-я** is removed and replaced by **-и**:

маса – мас**и**	ваканция – ваканци**и**
жена – жен**и**	нощ – нощ**и**

The neuter plural adds **-та** to the end of the word if it ends in **-е**:

куче – куче**та**	сокче – сокче**та**	яке – яке**та**

Neuter words ending in **-о** replace it by **-а**:

село – сел**а**	вино – вин**а**

If you want to specify a particular number of things then there is a special plural for masculine nouns only:

девет лимон**а** (NOT лимони)   два ча**я** (NOT чайове)
сто километр**а** (NOT километри) двеста грам**а** (NOT грамове)

This form is also used after the word **няколко** "several" or when you ask "how many?" **колко?**, for example: дайте ми няколко лимона, колко лимона искате?

When talking about more than one person, however, a special form of the number is used from 2 to 6 and the noun is in its standard masculine plural:

два стола   **двама** англичани
три сока   **трима** лекари

To say "many" and "much" in Bulgarian you need just one word: **много**
деца/пари many children/much money

Saying "the" and "a" (definite and indefinite articles)

Bulgarian is unusual in that "the" is not a separate word but is added to the end of the word to which it refers – either the noun or adjective (see below).

For the masculine **-ът**, or more rarely **-ят**, is added to the end of the word:

стол – столът   лекар – лекарят
мъж – мъжът   музей – музеят

There is also a shorter form of these, **-a** and **-я** respectively, when the noun is not the subject of the sentence:

дай ми **стола** give me the chair
покажете ми **музея** show me the museum

Note that in speech you will not hear the final **-т** anyway, so in both cases it will sound the same.

For feminine nouns the definite article is **-та**:

маса – масата   ваканция – ваканцията

For neuter nouns the definite article is **-то**, irrespective of the final vowel:

село – селото   куче – кучето   такси – таксито

The definite article for plural nouns depends on the final vowel in the plural form. For plurals ending in **-e** and **-и** it is **-те** (so the definite article is the same for both masculine and feminine):

лекари – лекарите   ръце – ръцете

For neuter or masculine nouns whose plural ends in **-a**, the definite article is **-та**:

села – селата   кучета – кучетата

Most often you don't need a word for "a" (indefinite article) in Bulgarian:
аз съм студент I'm a student

Sometimes, however, "a" is translated by the number "one": **един** (m), **една** (f), **едно** (n).

Properties: Adjectives and the verb "to be"

Adjectives have the same gender and number markers as the corresponding nouns. Please note that only masculine forms are listed in the dictionary.

Masculine	Feminine	Neuter	Plural
добър	добра	добро	добри
лек	лека	леко	леки

To say "more" and "most" of a certain property you put **по-** and **най-** in front of the adjective: **по-добър** better, **по-лек** lighter, **най-добър** best, **най-лек** lightest.

In definite descriptions the article is added to the end of the adjective and not to the noun, e.g. **хубавата жена** the beautiful woman. It is the same for nouns except in the masculine form:

Masculine	Feminine	Neuter	Plural
хубав**ият** мъж	хубав**ата** жена	хубав**ото** дете	хубав**ите** англичанки

When the adjective describes the noun by means of the verb "to be" then it still has to follow the gender and number of the noun:

лекарят е **добър** the doctor is good

детето е **умно** the child is clever

тревата е **зелена** the grass is green

жените са **хубави** the women are beautiful

So, you would say **ти си умен** (you are clever) to a man but **ти си умна** to a woman.

Passive participles are used as adjectives: **блокиран път** blocked road, **газирана вода** fizzy water, **отворени магазини** open shops. They form passive sentences with the verb "to be":

пътят е **блокиран** the road is blocked

аптеката е **затворена** the pharmacy is closed

The verb "to be":

	Present	Future	Simple past	Past progressive	Conditional	Imperative (command)	Past participle
аз	съм	ще съм/ бъда	бях	бях	бих		(m) бил (f) била (n) било
ти	си	ще си/ бъдеш	бе	беше	би	бъди	
той/ тя/то	е	ще е/ бъде	бе	беше	би		
ние	сме	ще сме/ бъдем	бяхме	бяхме	бихме	да бъдем	(pl) били
вие	сте	ще сте/ бъдете	бяхте	бяхте	бихте	бъдете	
те	са	ще са/ бъдат	бяха	бяха	биха		

Negation

To form negative statements just add the word for "no" **не** before the verb:
аз **не** съм студентка I'm not a student
тревата **не** е зелена the grass is not green

Some adjectives can form their opposites by adding **не** , too:
приятен pleasant   **не**приятен unpleasant
удобен comfortable   **не**удобен uncomfortable

The future tense of the verb *to be* has an irregular negative: **ще** is
substituted by **няма да** : утре **няма да** бъдем в хотела we're not going
to be in the hotel tomorrow.

Saying "how" and "to what extent": Adverbs

The regular way to make adverbs from adjectives is to use their neuter
form. For example, the adjective "fast" **бърз** as in **бърз влак** fast train
becomes **бързо** as in:
вие говорите много **бързо** you speak very fast

Adverbs are compared in the same way as adjectives: **моля, говорете
по-бавно**

Referring and pointing: Personal pronouns

	Subject	Direct object – short forms	Direct object – long forms	Indirect object – short forms	Indirect object – long forms
1st	аз I	ме me	мен(е) me	ми my	на мен(е) to me
2nd sg	ти you	те you	теб(е) you	ти your	на теб(е) to you
3rd m	той he	го him	него him	му his	на него to him
f	тя her	я her	нея her	и her	на нея to her
n	то it	го it	него it	му its	на него to it
1st pl	ние we	ни us	нас us	ни our	на нас to us
2nd pl	*вие you	*ви you	*вас you	*ви your	на *вас to you
3rd pl	те they	ги them	тях them	им their	на тях to them

*This is also the polite singular which in correspondence is written with an initial capital.

Transitive verbs take the direct object form and intransitive the indirect object form:

Иван **ме** вижда Ivan sees **me**　　= Иван вижда **мен** (with emphasis)

Иван **ми** говори Ivan is　　　　　= Иван говори **на мен** (with
talking **to me**　　　　　　　　　　　　emphasis)

Of course, some verbs take both a direct and an indirect object:

дай **му го** give **him it**　　　　　дай го **на него** give **it to him**

The long forms are used after prepositions (**на** to, **с** with, **до** next to, **за** for, **от** from, etc.), or for emphasis:

Иван говори **за тях** Ivan is talking about them

Иван говори **на мене** Ivan is talking to me

Frequently the subject pronoun is omitted unless you want to make a specific point:

виждам Елена I can see Elena　　　but　　　**аз** виждам Елена it's me
that can see Elena

Demonstrative pronouns

	m	f	n	pl
this	този	тази	това	тези
that	онзи	онази	онова	онези

Този is far more widely used than **онзи** and will often be used where in English we would use "that". So, for example, where in English we may point and say "can I have that box of chocolates please", in Bulgarian that would more frequently translate as **тази кутия бонбони, ако обичате**.

As a rule of thumb **онзи** refers to things at a considerable distance or to make a point that it is "that one over there" as opposed to "this one here".

Possession: Possessive adjectives and the verb "to have"

The most common way to say "my bag" in Bulgarian is the equivalent of "the bag to me", that is, to use the definite form of the noun and add the short form of the indirect object pronouns: **чантата ми**. Alternatively, you use possessive words like "my" and "mine" which agree in gender and number with the possessed item: **моята чанта**. Note that you need to use the article except after the verb "to be" : **чантата е моя**.

	Long form				Short form
Possessor	Possessed item				
	m	f	n	pl	
1st sg	мой	моя	мое	мои	ми
2nd sg	твой	твоя	твое	твои	ти
3rd sg	негов	негова	негово	негови	му
"one's own"	неин свой	нейна своя	нейно свое	нейни свои	и
					си
1st pl	наш	наша	наше	наши	ни
2nd pl	ваш	ваша	ваше	ваши	ви
3rd pl	техен	тяхна	тяхно	техни	им

The verb "to have"

Present	Future	Past	Imperfect	Conditional	Past participle	Imperative
имам	ще имам	имах	имах	бих + part.	(m) имал (f) имала (n) имало	
имаш	ще имаш	има	имаше	би		имай
има	ще има	има	имаше	би		
имаме	ще имаме	имахме	имахме	бихме	(pl) имали	да имаме
имате	ще имате	имахте	имахте	бихте		имайте
имат	ще имат	имаха	имаха	биха		

The negative of this verb is **нямам** "do not have" and it is formed in exactly the same way as **имам**.

Asking Questions

The main question words are:

кой? who?, which?

къде? where?

как? how?

каквo? what?

кога? when?

защо? why?

The following question words agree with the gender of the noun:

кой е този мъж? who's that man?

коя е тя? who's she?

кое дете? which child?

кои приятели? which friends?

какъв е той? who's he? (what's he like?)

каква е тя? what's she like?

какво е кафето? what sort of coffee is it?

какви са тези хора? who are those people?

To form a yes/no question without a question word you must use the word **ли**. The most difficult thing about asking **ли**-questions is deciding where to place it in the sentence, since it is moveable and comes immediately after the word/concept that is under question. So the same sentence can carry **ли** in different positions depending on exactly which element you focus on:

искаш **ли** кафе? do you **want** coffee?

кафе **ли** искаш? do you want **coffee**? (is it coffee you want or something else?)

ти **ли** искаш кафе? do **you** want coffee? (is it you that wants coffee or someone else?)

Identifying people and things: Relative pronouns and clauses

To say "the man who..." "the hotel which..." or "a room that..." you use words derived from the respective question word by adding - **то**:

Relative forms	m	f	n	pl
Identity	**който**	**която**	**което**	**които**
Characteristics	**какъвто**	**каквато**	**каквото**	**каквито**

мъжът, който е в стаята the man who's in the room

това не е стая, **каквато** исках this isn't the room (of the kind) I wanted

Describing actions: Verbs

The Bulgarian verb shows the person and number of the person doing the action, sometimes even the gender. There are three main types of verb based on the predominant vowel in the endings:

The Present Tense

	1st group (**-e**)		2nd group (**-и**)	3rd group (**-a** or **-я**)	
	пиша	живея	говоря	отивам	отговарям
	write	live	speak	go	answer
аз	пиша	живея	говоря	отивам	отговарям
ти	пишеш	живееш	говориш	отиваш	отговаряш
той/ тя/то	пише	живее	говори	отива	отговаря
ние	пишем	живеем	говорим	отиваме	отговаряме
вие	пишете	живеете	говорите	отивате	отговаряте
те	пишат	живеят	говорят	отиват	отговарят

There is no infinitive form of the verb in Bulgarian, so instead the form usually given in dictionaries (and in this book) is the "I" form (first person singular). In cases where you would use the infinitive "I want to…" you apply the word **да** followed by the respective person and number of the verb. For instance, "I want to live well" translates as **искам да живея добре**, but "he wants to live well" will be **той иска да живее добре**.

The Bulgarian verb is characterized by the notion of **aspect** or point of view. This means that most actions are represented by two verbs.

The **imperfective** aspect refers to actions that are in the process of being done, or else are repeated more than once or over a long period of time. All present tense actions, for instance, are "imperfective" because they are in the process of happening now, eg **отивам**.

The **perfective** verb of the pair refers to actions that are complete or momentary or performed only once, eg **да отида**. The perfective verbs cannot be used in the present unless they follow other verbs like "can, want, must" **мога, искам, трябва** with which they are linked by **да**, eg **трябва да отида** I have to go.

The distinction between the two verbs is marked in this book by adding **да** to the perfective one as a reminder that it cannot be used on its own. The dictionary lists both verbs for each action.

The Future Tense

The future is formed by using the word **ще** "will" plus the relevant aspect of the verb in the relevant person and number:

ще купим кола we're going to buy a car (perfective, you will only buy the car once)

от сега нататък аз ще купувам хляб from now on I will buy the bread (imperfective, you will buy it regularly).

For negative forms see Negation above.

Past Tenses: Simple past

This is formed mainly from perfective verbs. So if you want to say "I went", you have to choose the perfective verb of the pair of verbs with identical meaning, ie **да отида**. Imperfective verbs can also be viewed as having been completed in the past, eg "to speak, to live, to listen" below:

1st group -е			2nd group -и		3rd group -а
пиша	живея	да отида	говоря	да отговоря	слушам
to write	to live	to go	to speak	to answer	to listen
писах	живях	отидох	говорих	отговорих	слушах
писа	живя	отиде	говори	отговори	слуша
писа	живя	отиде	говори	отговори	слуша
писахме	живяхме	отидохме	говорихме	отговорихме	слушахме
писахте	живяхте	отидохте	говорихте	отговорихте	слушахте
писаха	живяха	отидоха	говориха	отговориха	слушаха

The Past Progressive

This is used when you refer to an event in the past that was going on at the moment when something else happened, or that went on for a long time. It combines most naturally with imperfective verbs:

Като малка живеех в Англия I lived in England when I was a child
Той често ми пишеше He wrote to me often

1st group -е		2nd group -и	3rd group -а	
пиша	живея	говоря	отивам	отговарям
to write	to live	to speak	to go	to answer
пишех	живеех	говорех	отивах	отговарях
пишеше	живееше	говореше	отиваше	отговаряше

пишеше	живееше	говореше	отиваше	отговаряше
пишехме	живеехме	говорехме	отивахме	отговаряхме
пишехте	живеехте	говорехте	отивахте	отговаряхте
пишеха	живееха	говореха	отиваха	отговаряха

The Present Perfect

This tense corresponds to the English "I have lived in Varna" **аз съм живяла във Варна**. It is used to describe the result of actions without specifying necessarily when they were completed. To form this tense you need the present tense of the verb "to be" (see above) plus the past participle (see below). For example:

тя е живяла в Англия she has lived in England
говорили сме с него we've talked to him

The Past Participle

Past Participles are used to build complex tenses and the conditional. They are formed from the past simple or past progressive forms by replacing the personal endings with **л** (m), **ла** (f), **ло** (n), **ли** (pl): the past tense form **говорих** becomes **говорил**.

Commands, warnings and requests: Imperative and Conditional forms

Many of the polite formulas in Bulgarian are actually imperative, eg **Заповядайте!** Here you are/Take a seat!, **Здравейте!** Hello! (literally Be healthy!), **Кажете!** How can I help you? (literally Say!).

Number	1st group -е да спра to stop	2nd group -и говоря to speak	3rd group -а внимавам to watch out
singular	спри!	говори!	внимавай!
plural	спрете!	говорете!	внимаваите!

There are also some irregular forms of very common verbs:
give: **дай! дайте!** (from the verb да дам)   come: **ела! елате!**
look: **виж! вижте!** (from the verb да видя)

Warnings (ie negative imperatives) can only be formed from imperfective verbs. So, if you have a positive form "stop!" **спри!** (from the verb да), the negative "don't stop!" will be **не спирай!** (from the verb спирам). Warnings are also frequently formed with the help of the word **недей!**

недейте! plus the usual present tense form introduced by **да**, eg: don't speak! **недей да** говориш!/(sg) **недейте да** говорите! (pl)

For polite requests you can use the special conditional form:
Би ли отворил прозореца? (m) **Би ли** отворила прозореца? (f)
Бихте ли отворили прозореца? (pl)
For the forms of the conditional see the tables below.

Two frequently used verbs

To want

Present	Future	Past	Imperfect	Conditional	Past participle	Imperative
искам	ще искам	исках	исках	бих искал искала	*(m)* искал	
искаш	ще искаш ще иска ще	иска	искаше	би искал	*(f)* искала	искай
иска		иска	искаше	би искал	*(n)* искало	
искаме	искаме ще искате ще искат	искахме	искахме	бихме искали	*(pl)* искали	да искаме
искате		искахте	искахте	бихте искали		искайте
искат		искаха	искаха	биха искали		

Can

мога	ще мога	можах	можех	бих могъл могла	*(m)* могъл *(f)* могла *(n)* могло	
	ще можеш ще може ще можем ще можете ще могат					
можеш		можа	можеше	би могъл		
може		можа	можеше	би могъл		
можем		можахме	можехме	бихме могли	*(pl)* могли	
можете		можахте	можехте	бихте могли		
могат		можаха	можеха	биха могли		

GRAMMAR

HOLIDAYS AND FESTIVALS

National holidays are known as **празници** *praznitsi*. Administrative offices and banks are closed, as are most museums, shops and offices.

1 Jan	**Нова година** *(Nova godeena)*, New Year's Day, in the villages children go around patting people's backs with a stick decorated with dried fruit and popcorn, called a **сурвачка** *soorvachka*: this is supposed to bring luck and health for the coming year.
3 March	**Освобождение на България от турско робство** *(Osvobozhdeni-eh na Bulgari-ya ot toorsko ropstvo)*, Liberation Day: national holiday commemorating the end of the Ottoman occupation (1396–1878)
March–April	**Великден** *(Veleekden)*, Easter. Date varies according to the Orthodox calendar. Easter Monday is a holiday. Traditionally, people paint **великденски яйца** *veleekdenski yaytsa* (Easter eggs) and make **козунаци** *kozoonatsi* (plaited brioche loaves). The loaves are blessed at Mass and there is a procession around the church carrying icons. Families get together for a meal and play a traditional game where people knock hard-boiled eggs together: whoever breaks their opponent's egg without damaging their own will enjoy good health for the rest of the year.
1 May	**Ден на труда** *(Den na trooduh)*, International Labour Day.
6 May	**Гергьовден** *(Gergyovden)*, St George's day, patron saint of shepherds. Traditionally, early spring rituals believed to bring prosperity were performed. Since 1999, this has also been a holiday in honour of the Bulgarian Army.
24 May	**Ден на българската просвета, култура и славянската писменост** *(Den na bulgarskata prosveta, kooltoora ee slavyanskata peesmenost)*, Slavic education, culture and literature day. A day in honour of St Cyril and St Methodius, the brothers credited with inventing the Cyrillic alphabet, on which various cultural events are organized.
6 Sept	**Ден на Съединението** *(Den na Su-edineni-eto)*, Union Day, celebrating the 1885 union of the principality of Bulgaria with the province of Eastern Rumelia.

22 Sept	**Ден на Независимостта** (*Den na Nezavisimosta*), Independence Day, celebrating King Ferdinand's 1908 declaration of Bulgaria's independence from the Ottoman Empire.
1 Nov	**Ден на будителите** (*Den na boodeetelite*), Enlighteners' Day, in honour of the teachers who revived the Bulgarian national pride during the 19th century Bulgarian Renaissance.
24 Dec	**Бъдни вечер** (*Budni vecher*), Christmas Eve is the more important celebration in Bulgaria. It is the last day of the pre-Christmas fast and in the evening all family members gather around the table with either 7 or 9 ritual vegan dishes, such as bean stew, peppers and cabbage leaves stuffed with rice and sultanas. A large round bread (**погача** *pogacha*) is broken into pieces by the family elder and each family member receives a piece. Whoever gets the coin hidden in the bread will have wealth and luck the coming year. Each person breaks a walnut to see their fortune for the year ahead: a good nut foretells a good year.
25-26 Dec	**Коледа** (*Koleda*), Christmas. In villages, groups of young boys called **коледари** *Koledari* go from house to house singing songs of good wishes, receiving small gifts and sweets in return.

The main festivals and celebrations

6 January	**Богоявление** (*Bogoyavleni-eh*), commemoration of the baptism of Christ in the river Jordan: traditional rituals involving water are performed. A cross is thrown into the nearest river and young men dive in to catch it.
14 February	**Трифон Зарезан** (*Treefon Zarezan*), a wine festival: a branch must be cut from the nearest vine "so that the harvest will be good this year", and a big meal is provided on the village square.
March	Singing competition in Varna; March Music Days in Ruse.
1 March	**Баба Марта** (*Baba Marta*), a celebration of the coming of spring. People give each other a **мартеница** (*martenitsa*) made of red and white threads (symbolising life and purity), which they pin to their clothing as a good luck token, and wish each other **Честита баба марта** *chesteeta baba marta*

("happy Grandma March"). The token is only removed when spring has well and truly arrived (blossom comes out, the storks return etc), and is placed under a stone or tied to a fruit tree.

early March **Кукери** (*Kookeri*), a carnival parade held in many villages and some towns on the first Sunday of March. Locals in grotesque masks and costumes parade nosily through the streets with sheep's bells at their belts.

8 March **Ден на жената** (*Den na zhenata*), International Women's Day. This is widely celebrated in Bulgaria and men give their wives and female colleagues flowers.

March (Lent) **Тодоровден** (*Todorovden*), a horse festival held on the first Saturday of Lent. Icons of St Theodore, protector of horses, are carried through the streets on a white horse, and various sporting events involving horses take place.

Цветница (*Tsvetnitsa*), a day of flowers, held on Palm Sunday. People go to church with willow branches and take their blessing.

May–June **Sofia Music Weeks**, musical events are held at various locations throughout the city and include guest performers from abroad.

1 June **Ден на детето** (*Den na deteto*), Children's Day: various cultural and artistic events are organized for children.

June–August **Варненско лято** (*Varnensko lyato*), Varna Summer: this festival created in 1926 features theatre and many types of music.

July International ballet competition in Varna.
Festival of Gypsy Music and Songs in Stara Zagora.

August **Bansko Jazz Festival**.
Koprivshtista Folklore Festival, held every five years.
Пирин пее (*Peerin pe-eh*) "the Pirin mountains sing", a traditional music festival in the south-west of Bulgaria.

September Apolonia Arts Festival in Sozopol.

26 October **Димитровден** (*Dimeetrovden*), St Dimiter's day, marking the beginning of winter: it is believed that if the first person to visit you that day is a good person, the winter will be mild and the year prosperous.

8 December **Студентски празник** (*Stoodentski praznik*), Students' Day: universities are closed.

USEFUL ADDRESSES

Before your trip, you may wish to consult the following websites (both in English):
http://www.bulgariatravel.org/
http://www.tourism-bulgaria.com

The Bulgarian Embassy website (http://www.bulgarianembassy.org.uk/) also offers some tourist information and useful links.

In the UK
Embassy of the Republic of Bulgaria
186-188 Queen's Gate, London SW7 5HL
Tel.: 0207 584 9400, 0207 5849 433
Fax: 0207 584 4948
Website: http://www.bulgarianembassy.org.uk/

In the US
Embassy of the Republic of Bulgaria, Washington, DC
1621 22nd Street, NW, Washington DC 20008
Tel.: (202) 387 0174
Fax: (202) 234 7973
Website: http://www.bulgaria-embassy.org/

In Bulgaria
British Embassy, Sofia
9 Moskovska Street, Sofia 1000
Tel.: (00359) (2) 933 9222
Fax: (00359) (2) 933 92 50
E-mail: britembinf@mail.orbitel.bg

British Honorary Consul, Varna
40 Graf Ignatiev Street, PO Box 229, Varna
Tel.: (00359) (52) 6655 555
Fax: (00359) (52) 6655 755
E-mail: nikolai.bozhilov@unimasters.com

Embassy of the United States, Sofia
16, Kozyak Street, Sofia 1407
Tel.: (00359) (2) 937 5100
Fax: (00359) (2) 937 5320
E-mail: sofia@usembassy.bg
Website: www.bulgaria.usembassy.gov

Directory enquiries: 144
Medical emergencies: 150
Police: 166
Fire brigade: 160

CONVERSION TABLES

Note that when writing numbers, Bulgarian uses either a comma or a full stop where English uses a full stop. For example 0.6 could be written 0,6 in Bulgarian. Thousands, millions etc are marked with a space only: 3 000, 1 000 000.

MEASUREMENTS

Only the metric system is used in Bulgaria.

Length
1 cm ≈ 0.4 inches
30 cm ≈ 1 foot

Distance
1 metre ≈ 1 yard
1 km ≈ 0.6 miles

To convert kilometres into miles, divide by 8 and then multiply by 5.

kilometres	1	2	5	10	20	100
miles	0.6	1.25	3.1	6.25	12.50	62.5

To convert miles into kilometres, divide by 5 and then multiply by 8.

miles	1	2	5	10	20	100
kilometres	1.6	3.2	8	16	32	160

Weight
25g ≈ 1 oz   1 kg ≈ 2 lb   6 kg ≈ 1 stone

To convert kilos into pounds, divide by 5 and then multiply by 11.
To convert pounds into kilos, multiply by 5 and then divide by 11.

kilos	1	2	10	20	60	80
pounds	2.2	4.4	22	44	132	176

Liquid
1 litre ≈ 2 pints
4.5 litres ≈ 1 gallon

Temperature
To convert temperatures in Fahrenheit into Celsius, subtract 32, multiply by 5 and then divide by 9.

To convert temperatures in Celsius into Fahrenheit, divide by 5, multiply by 9 and then add 32.

Fahrenheit (°F)	32	40	50	59	68	86	100
Celsius (°C)	0	4	10	15	20	30	38

Clothes sizes

Sometimes you will find sizes given using the English-language abbreviations **XS** (Extra Small), **S** (Small), **M** (Medium), **L** (Large) and **XL** (Extra Large).

• Women's clothes

Bulgarian sizes are calculated on the basis of the bust and hip circumference divided in two. In general, this makes 6 units more than the European standard, eg European 44 would correspond to Bulgarian 50.

Europe	36	38	40	42	44	etc
UK	8	10	12	14	16	
Bulgarian	42	44	46	48	50	

• Bras (Bulgaria uses the European sizes)

Europe	70	75	80	85	90	etc
UK	32	34	36	38	40	

• Men's shirts (Bulgaria uses the same collar sizes as Europe)

Europe	36	37	38	39	41	42	43	etc
UK	14	141/2	15	151/2	16	161/2	17	

• Men's clothes (again, Bulgaria follows the European system)

Europe	40	42	44	46	48	50	etc
UK	30	32	34	36	38	40	

Shoe sizes

• Women's shoes

Europe	37	38	39	40	42	etc
UK	4	5	6	7	8	

• Men's shoes

Europe	40	42	43	44	46	etc
UK	7	8	9	10	11	